Questions & Answers SCIENCE

First published in 2016 by Miles Kelly Publishing Ltd
Harding's Barn, Bardfield End Green, Thaxted, Essex, CM6 3PX, UK

2 4 6 8 10 9 7 5 3 1

Publishing Director Belinda Gallagher
Creative Director Jo Cowan
Editors Fran Bromage, Sarah Parkin, Claire Philip
Designers Jo Cowan, Rob Hale, Andrea Slane
Cover Designer Simon Lee
Production Elizabeth Collins, Caroline Kelly
Reprographics Stephan Davis, Jennifer Barker, Thom Allaway

ISBN 978-1-78209-973-4

Printed in China

British Library Cataloguing-in-Publication Data
A catalogue record for this book is available from the British Library

ACKNOWLEDGEMENTS
The publishers would like to thank the following for the use of their photographs:
Front cover GustoImages/Science Photo Library (robot), mickeyd_600/iStock (butterfly), Elena Elisseeva/Shutterstock (flower) **Back cover** Linda Bucklin/Shutterstock
Getty 72 Lowell Georgia/Getty Images
Shutterstock.com 1 takasu; 3 XYZ; 4-5 mtr; 6 Sergey Lavrentev; 7 Monkey Business Images; 8 Wade H. Massie; 10 XYZ; 11 Chris Parypa Photography; 13 Pavel L Photo and Video; 14-15 takasu; 15 Snowbelle; 16 ThomBal; 17 Creative Travel Projects; 18(br) tratong, (c) tratong; 19 qingqing; 20-21 ifong; 22-23(c) Anton Balazh, (tr) scyther5; 24 Natursports; 26 Alexander Raths; 29 Aditya Singh; 31 Hurst Photo; 34-35 Frederick R. Matzen; 37 Sergey Novikov; 38-39 Tomasz Trojanowski; 40 Sergey Novikov; 41 TungCheung; 42 Ralf Juergen Kraft; 44-45 Frederick R. Matzen; 45 Jaren Jai Wicklund; 46-47 Alila Medical Media; 47 SpeedKingz; 48-49 Elena Schweitzer; 49 Vinicius Tupinamba; 57 Ermolaev Alexander; 59 beerkoff; 60-61 Ljupco Smokovski; 61 picturepartners; 64-65 Volodymyr Golnyk; 70-71 Mopic; 71(tr) beboy, (bl) Bjartur Snorrason; 73 airphoto.gr; 75 Galyna Andrushko; 77(tl) Menna, (tc) Joseph Sohm, (tr) yankane; 78 Shutterstock; 79 Sergey Nivens; 80 Vadim Petrakov; 81 zschnepf; 83(tr) Cloudia Spinner, (cl) Rich Carey; 85(tr) Filip Fuxa, (tl) douglas knight; 86-87 Patrick Poendl; 89 Minerva Studio; 90 Fedorov Oleksiy; 91(cr) oliveromg, (bl) Stephen Meese

All other photographs are from:
digitalSTOCK, digitalvision, Image State, John Foxx, PhotoAlto, PhotoDisc, PhotoEssentials, PhotoPro, Stockbyte

All artworks from the Miles Kelly Artwork Bank

Every effort has been made to acknowledge the source and copyright holder of each picture. Miles Kelly Publishing apologizes for any unintentional errors or omissions.

Made with paper from a sustainable forest

www.mileskelly.net info@mileskelly.net

Contents

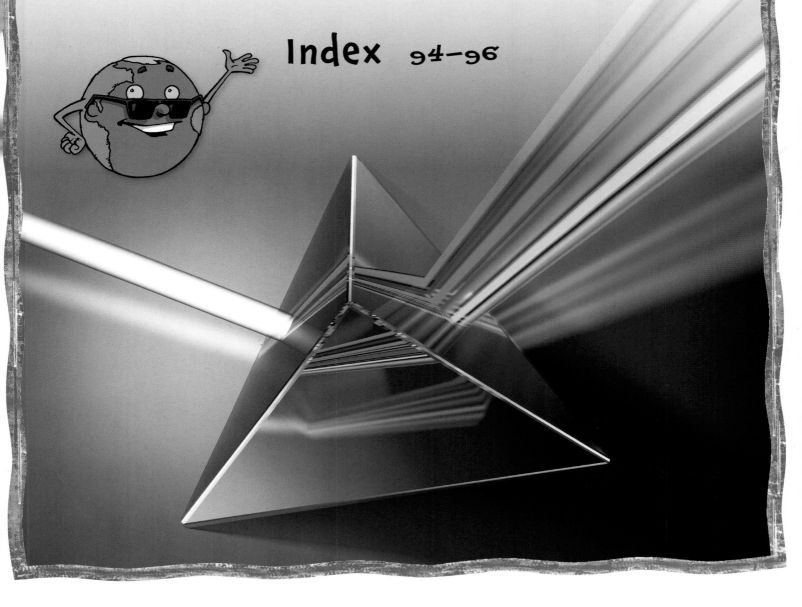

Science

Is science in the playground?

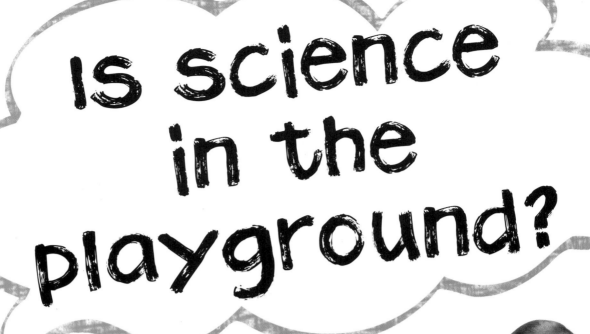

Yes, it is! Lots of science happens in a playground. The playground rides could not work without science. A see-saw is a simple machine called a lever. It has a long arm and a point in the middle called a pivot. As you ride on the see-saw, the lever tips up and down on the pivot.

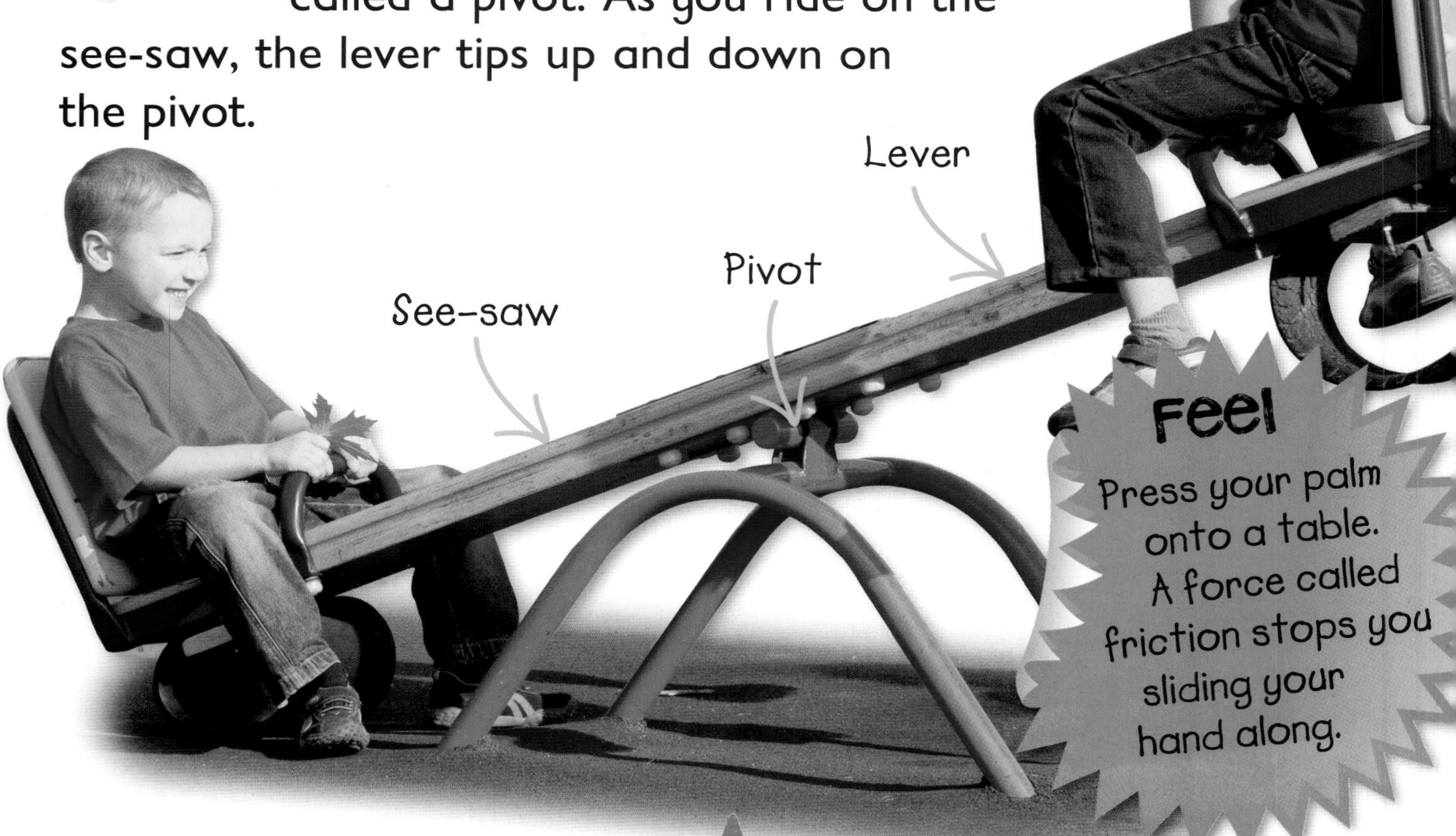

Feel

Press your palm onto a table. A force called friction stops you sliding your hand along.

What is a wheel?

A wheel is a very simple machine that can spin around. Wheels let other machines, such as skateboards, bicycles, cars and trains, roll along smoothly. They also make it easy to move heavy weights in carts and wheelbarrows.

Riding bikes

Sloping machine

A ramp is the simplest machine of all. It is easier to walk up a ramp to the top of a hill than it is to climb a steep hillside.

What makes things stop and start?

Pushes and pulls make things stop and start. Scientists use the word 'force' for pushes and pulls. Forces are all around us. The force of gravity pulls things downwards. It makes a rollercoaster car hurtle downhill. It also slows the car on the uphill parts of the track.

Rollercoaster

why do fireworks flash and bang?

Fireworks flash and bang because they are full of chemicals that burn. The chemicals have lots of energy stored in them. When they burn, the energy changes to light, heat and sound. We use chemicals that burn in other places too, such as cookers, heaters and car engines.

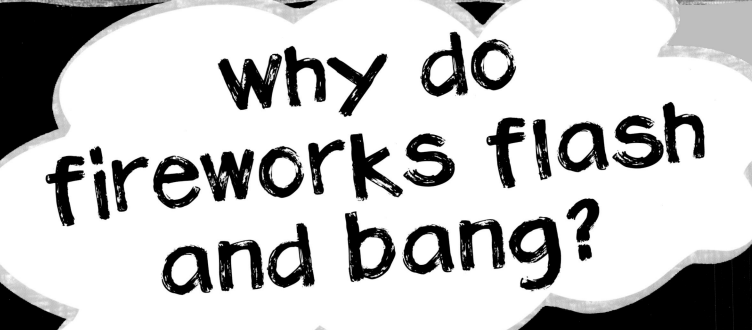

Fireworks

How do candles burn?

Candles are made of wax and a wick (string). When the wick is lit, the wax around it melts. The wick then soaks up the liquid wax and the heat of the flame turns the wax into a gas (vapour), which burns away. As the wax becomes vapour it cools the wick, allowing the candle to burn slowly.

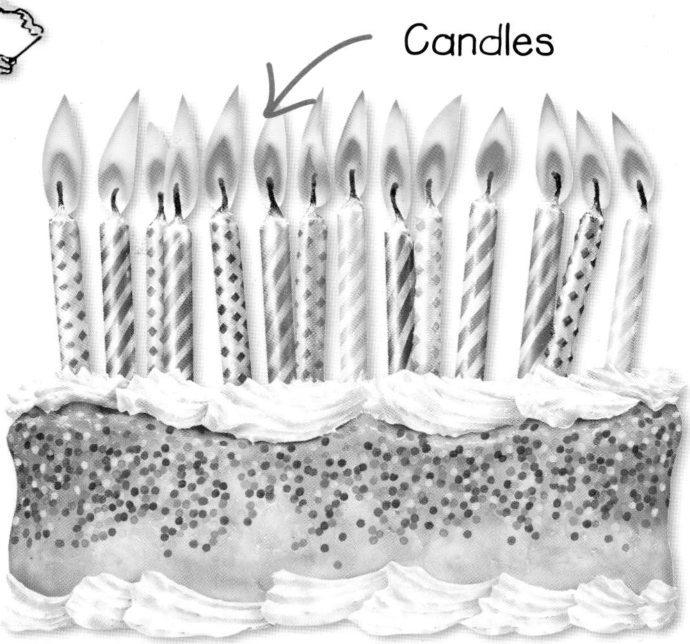

Hot! Hot! Hot!

The hottest-ever temperature recorded was in a science laboratory. It was four hundred million degrees Celsius (400,000,000°C).

Remember

Which piece of equipment is used to measure how hot or cold something is?

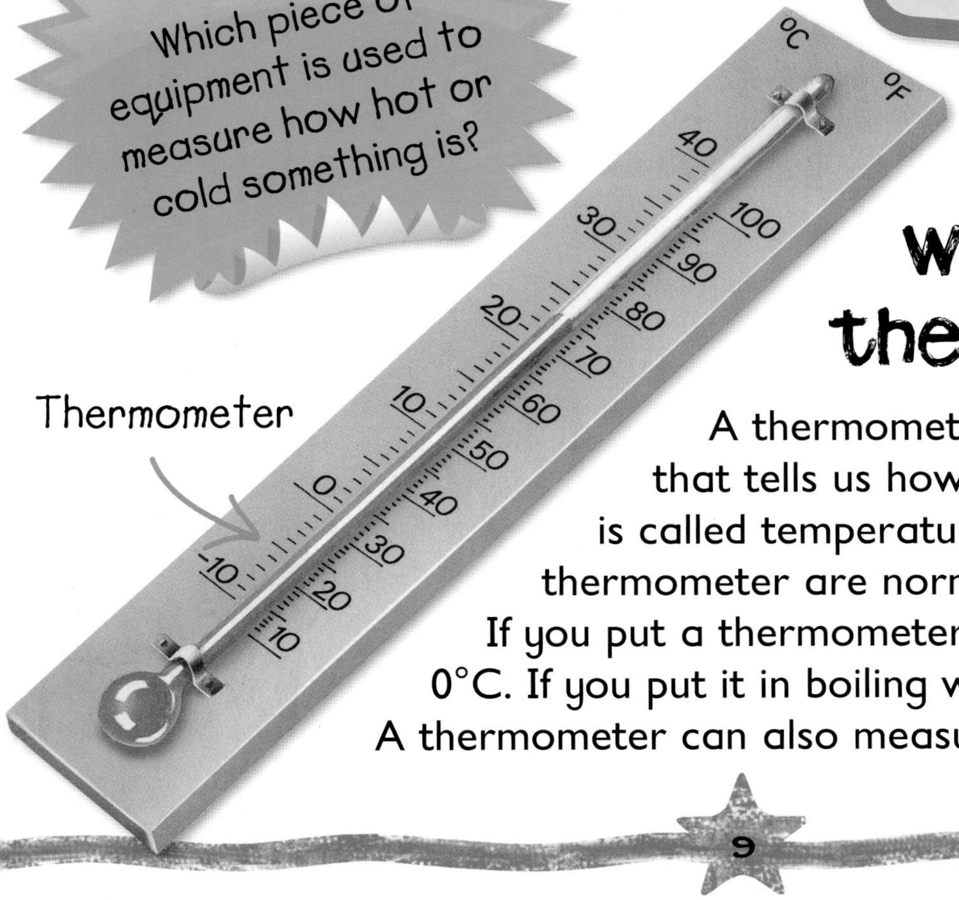

What is a thermometer?

A thermometer is an instrument that tells us how hot something is. This is called temperature. The numbers on a thermometer are normally degrees Celsius (°C). If you put a thermometer in cold water, it shows 0°C. If you put it in boiling water it shows 100°C. A thermometer can also measure body temperature.

How does light bend?

Light rays travel in straight lines. When light shines through a prism, the rays bend because light travels more slowly through glass than air. Sunlight is called white light, but it is made up of a mixture of colours. When white light passes through a prism it splits into many colours, like a rainbow.

Make

On a sunny day, stand with your back to the Sun. Spray water into the air and you should see a rainbow!

Fast as light

Light is the fastest thing in the Universe. It travels 300,000 kilometres every second. That means it could travel around the Earth seven times in less than a second!

What is the loudest sound?

The roar of a jet engine is the loudest sound we normally hear. It is thousands of times louder than someone shouting. Sounds this loud can damage our ears if we are too close to them.

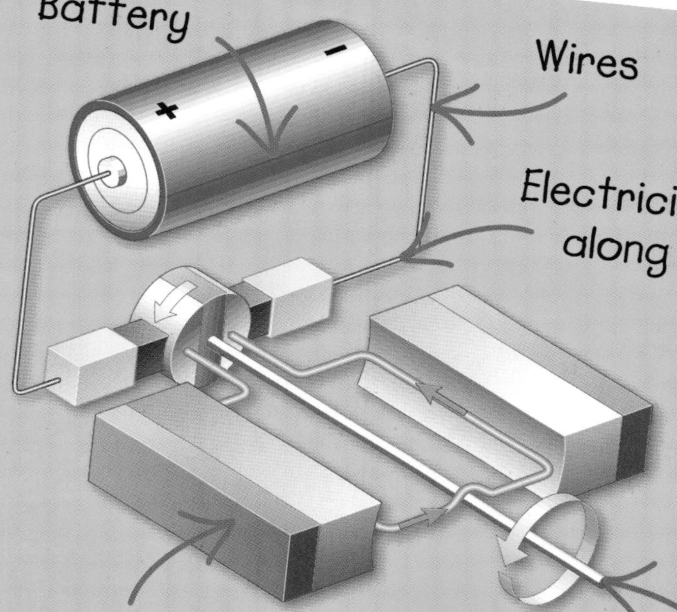

What is inside an electric motor?

Magnets and wires are inside an electric motor. Electricity from a battery passes through the wires, which turns the wires into a magnet. Two more magnets on each side of the motor push and pull against the wires. This makes a thin metal rod (spindle) spin around.

Where is science in a city?

Everywhere! In a big city, almost every machine, building and vehicle is based on science. Cars, buses and trains help us move around the city. Scientists and engineers have also worked out how to build tall skyscrapers where people live and work.

Spot

Look at this city picture. How many different forms of transport can you spot?

Railway signals

Who works railway signals?

Nobody does – the signals work by themselves. Electronic parts on the track work out if a train is passing. Then a computer changes the signals to red, to stop another train moving onto the same piece of track.

How do skyscrapers stay up?

Skyscrapers stay up because they have a strong frame on the inside. The frame is made from steel and concrete. These are very strong materials. Normally you can't see the frame. It is hidden by the skyscraper's walls. The walls hang on the frame.

Plane spotters

There's science at an airport, too. A radar machine uses radio waves to find aircraft in the sky. This helps people at the airport to guide the aircraft onto the runway.

Skyscrapers

How do you make magnets?

By using another magnet. Magnets are made from lumps of iron or steel. You can turn a piece of iron into a magnet by stroking it with another magnet.

A magnet can also be made by sending electricity through a coil of wire. This is called an electromagnet. Some electromagnets are so strong, they can pick up cars.

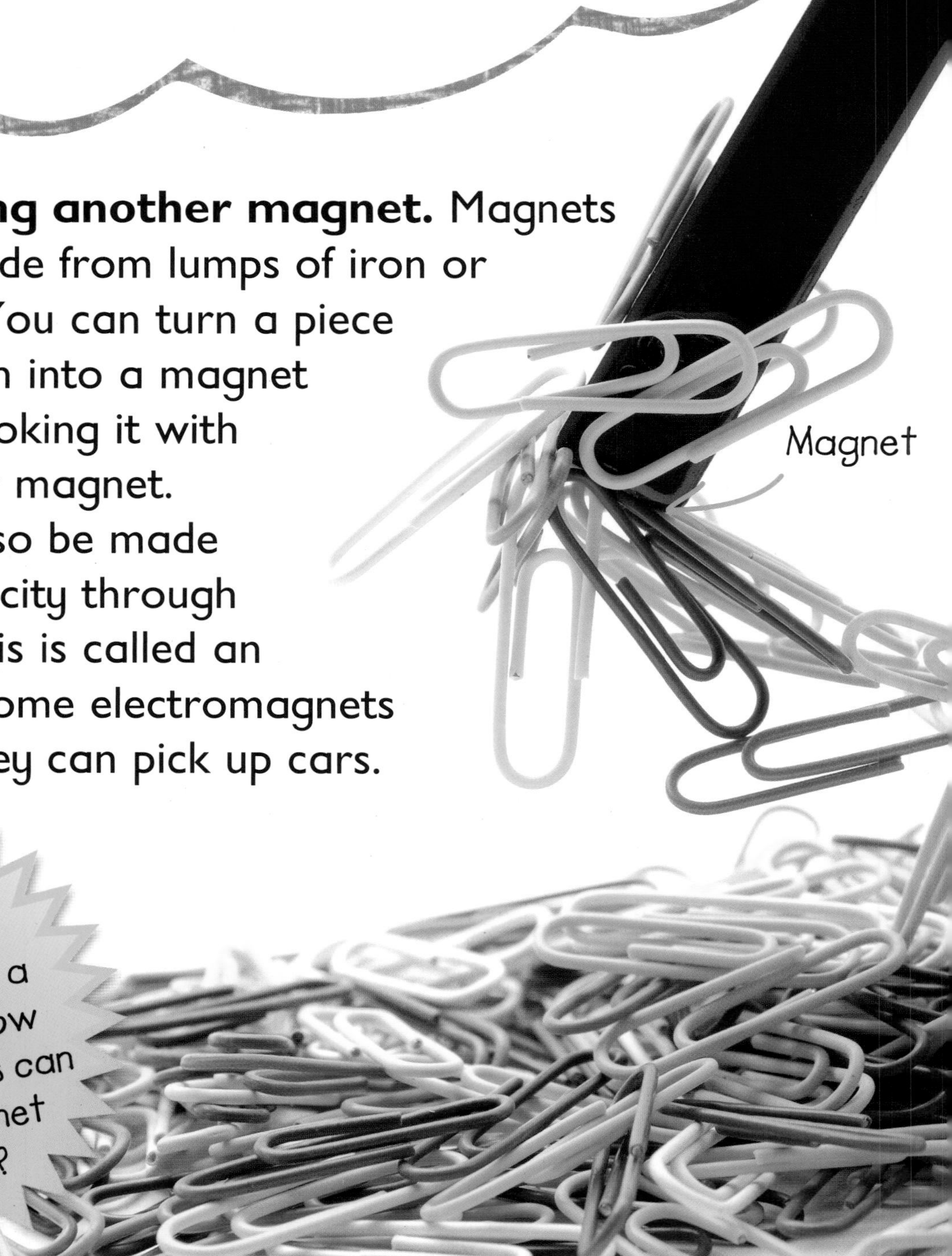

Count

Find a magnet at home (you can use a fridge magnet). How many paper clips can your magnet pick up?

Does a magnet have a field?

Yes – but it's not a field of grass. The area around a magnet is called a magnetic field. A magnetic field is shown by drawing lines around a magnet. The Earth has a magnetic field, too. It is as though there is a giant magnet inside the Earth.

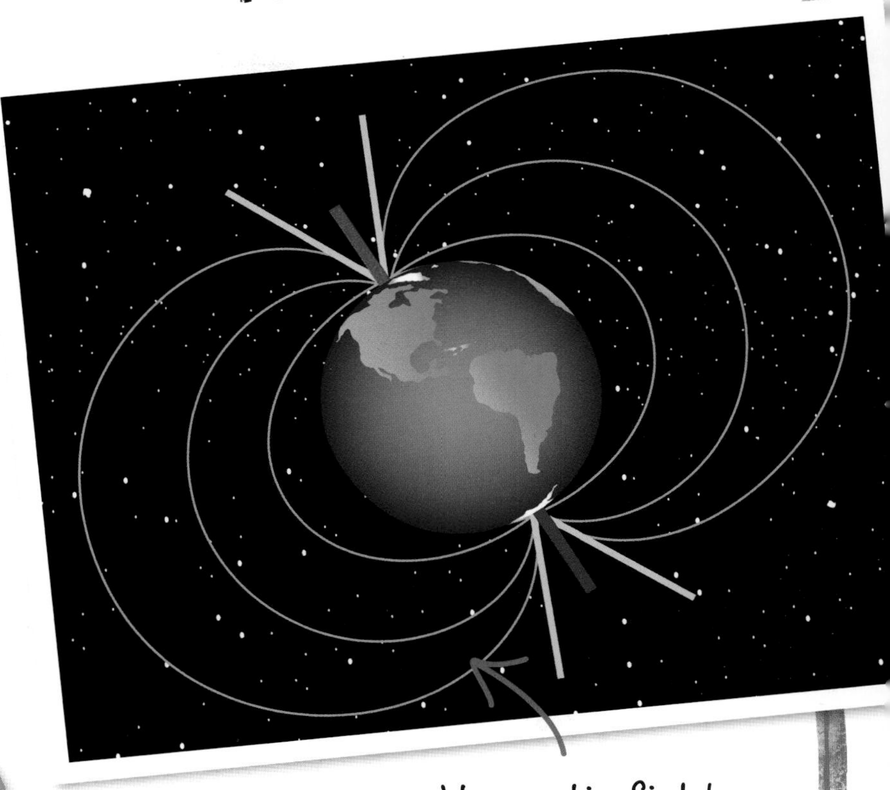

Magnetic field

Handy rock

Some rocks act like magnets. Years ago, people used magnetic rocks to find their way. If they let the rock spin round, it always pointed in the same direction.

What are poles?

Every magnet has two poles. These are where the pull of a magnet is strongest. They are called the north pole and the south pole. A north pole and a south pole always pull towards each other. Two north poles always push each other away. So do two south poles.

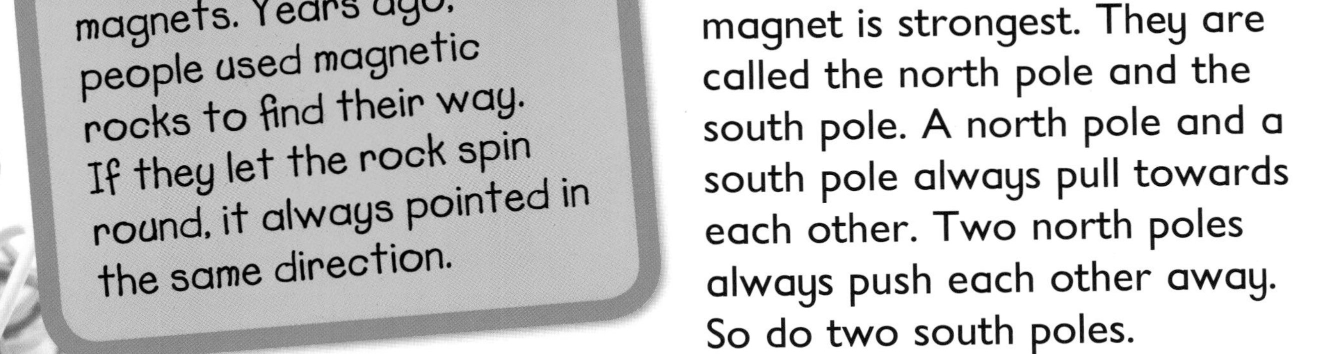

Where does electricity come from?

Electricity comes to your home along cables from power stations. The cables are held off the ground by pylons. Around your home are holes in the wall called sockets. When a machine is plugged into a socket, electricity flows out to work the machine.

Excellent electric

Our homes are full of machines that use a lot of electricity. If we didn't have access to electricity we wouldn't have televisions, lights, washing machines or computers!

When is electricity in the sky?

When there's a thunderstorm. During a storm, a kind of electricity called static electricity builds up, which can make a big flash, that lights up the sky. This is lightning. The hot lightning heats up the air around it, which makes a loud clap. This is thunder.

What is a circuit?

A circuit is a loop that electricity moves around. This circuit is made up of a battery, a light bulb and a switch. If the switch is turned off, the loop would be broken. Then the electricity would stop moving and the light would go out.

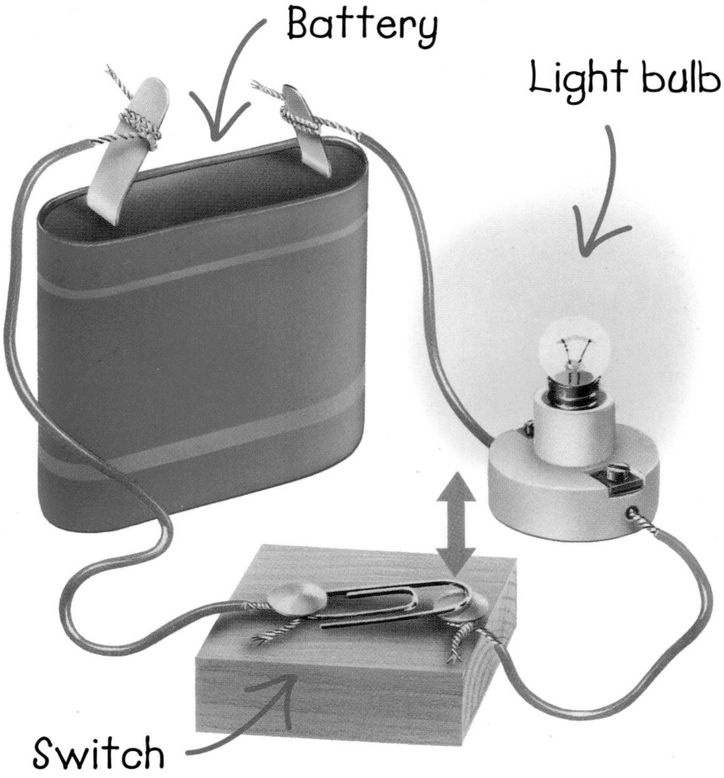

Remember

Mains electricity is dangerous. It could kill you. Never play with sockets in your home.

What waves are invisible?

Radio waves are all around us, but we can't see them. We use radio waves to send sounds and pictures to radios and televisions. Some radio waves come from satellites in space. A radio set receives radio waves through a metal rod called an aerial. A dish-shaped aerial picks up radio waves for television programmes.

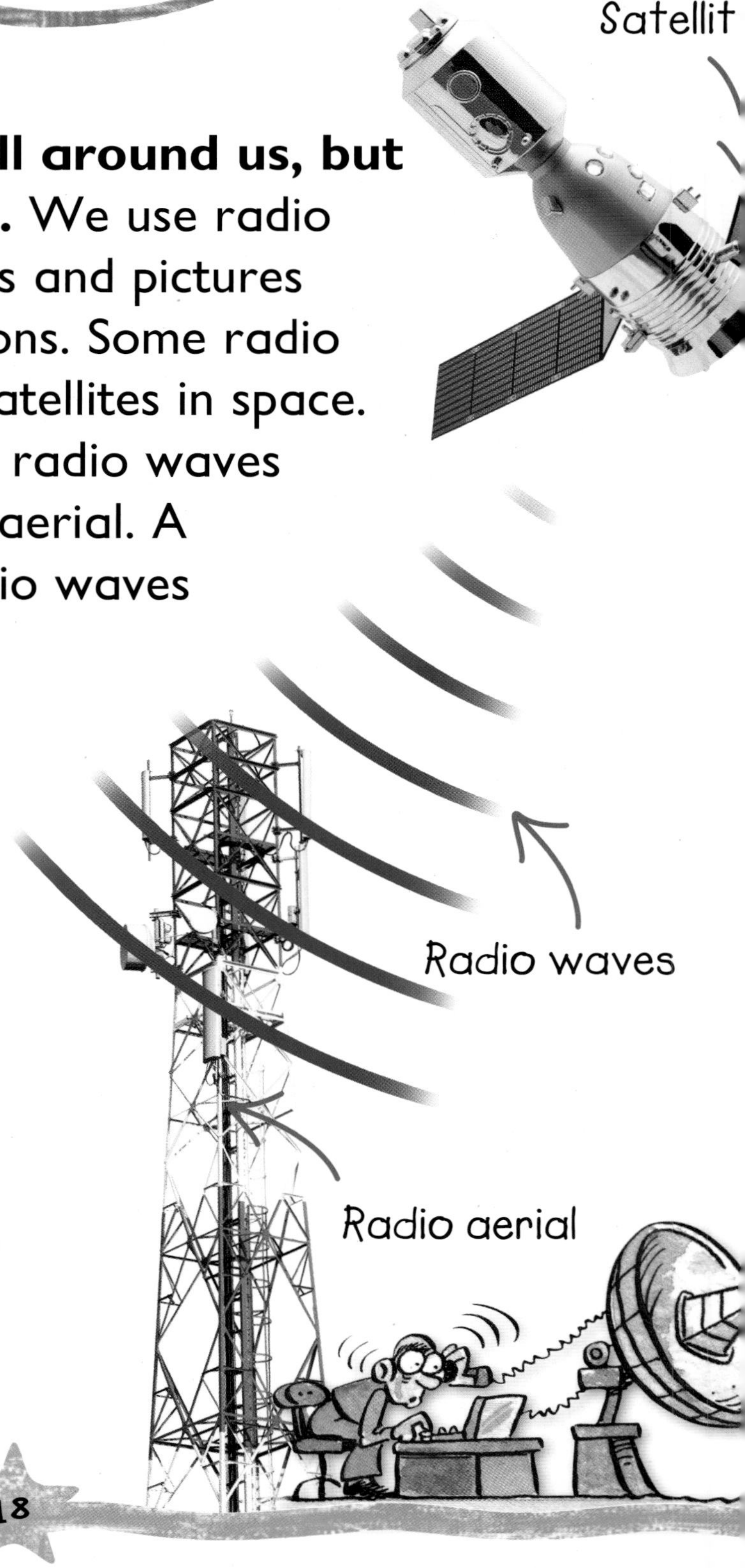

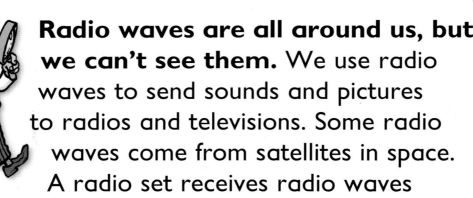

Space radio

Radio waves can travel through space. But they can't travel through water. So you can listen to a radio in a space station, but not in a submarine!

What is an X-ray?

An X-ray is like a radio wave. X-rays can go through the soft bits of your body. However, hard bones stop them. That's why doctors use X-ray machines to take pictures of the inside of people's bodies.

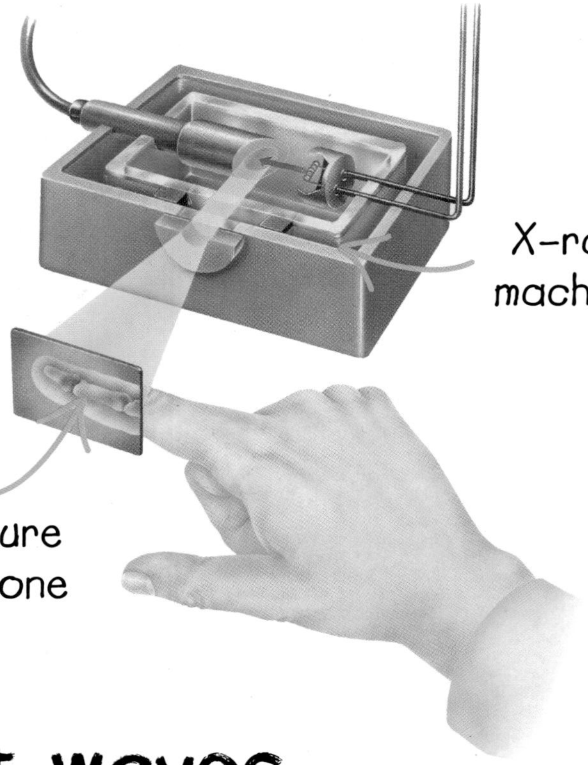

Remember

Which part of your body would stop an X-ray? Skin or bone?

What waves can cook food?

Microwaves can. These are a kind of radio wave. They have lots of energy in them. A microwave uses this energy to cook food. Microwaves are fired into the oven. They make the particles in the food jiggle about. This makes the food hot.

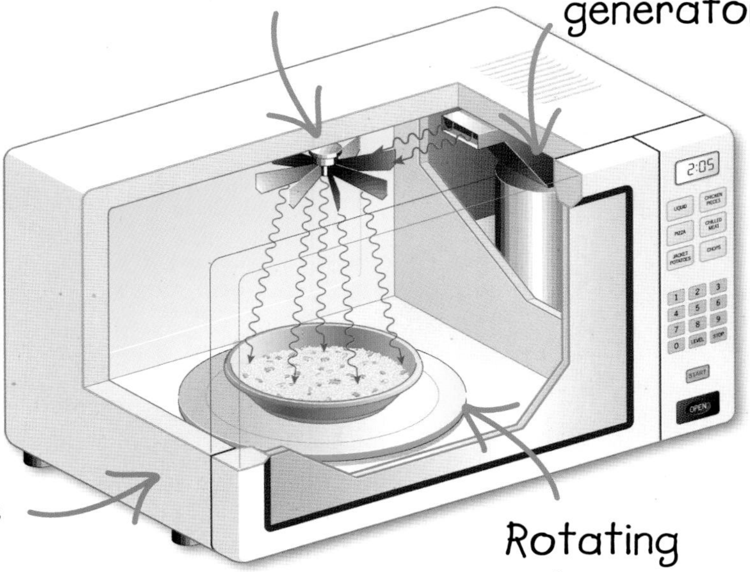

Are computers clever?

Not really. Computers are amazing machines, but they can only do what they are told. They carry out computer programs written by people. These are full of instructions that the computer follows. You can also tell a computer what to do by using its keyboard and mouse.

Read

What is the name of a computer's electronic brain? Read these pages again to help you find out.

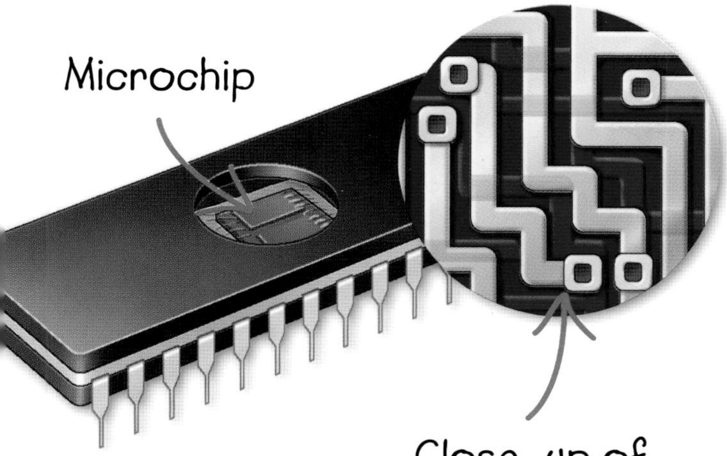

Does a computer have a brain?

A computer doesn't have a brain like yours. It has an electronic brain called a central processing unit. This is a microchip the size of your fingernail, and it can do millions of difficult calculations in a split second.

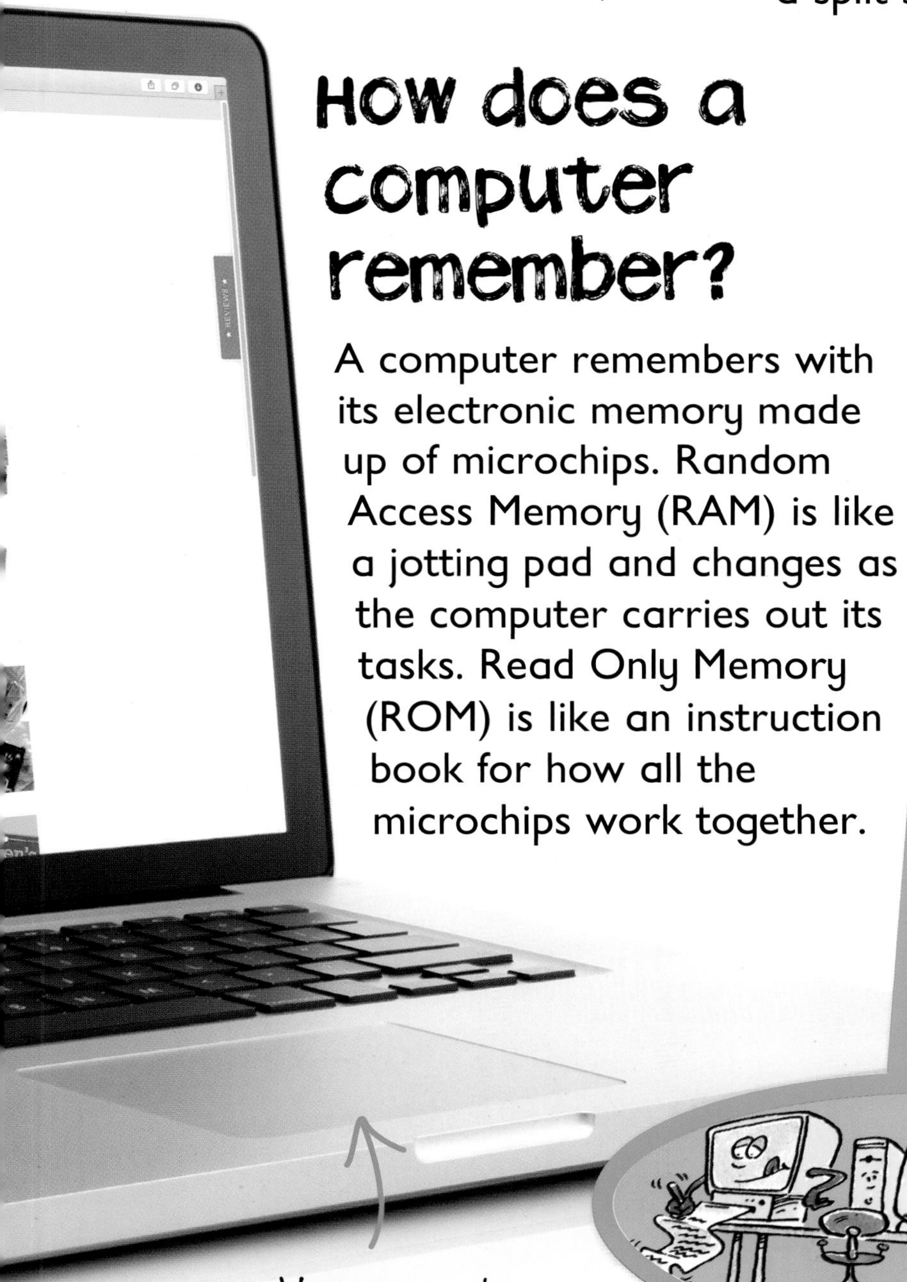

How does a computer remember?

A computer remembers with its electronic memory made up of microchips. Random Access Memory (RAM) is like a jotting pad and changes as the computer carries out its tasks. Read Only Memory (ROM) is like an instruction book for how all the microchips work together.

Computer room

The first computer was made 70 years ago. It was so big that it filled a whole room and weighed almost 50 tonnes.

How is the Internet like a web?

The Internet is made up of millions of computers around the world. They are connected like a giant spider's web! A computer connects to a machine called a modem. This sends signals to a server. The server lets you connect to the Internet. People can send emails and open web pages.

Find out

Use the Internet, with a grown-up, to find out who invented the World Wide Web.

What does www stand for?

The letters www are short for World Wide Web. The World Wide Web is like a giant library of information, stored on computers all over the world. There are also thousands of shops on the World Wide Web, where you can buy almost anything.

Can I use the Internet without a computer?

Yes. Other machines like mobile phones can link to the Internet, so you can find out information and send and receive emails too. A mobile phone connects to the Internet by radio.

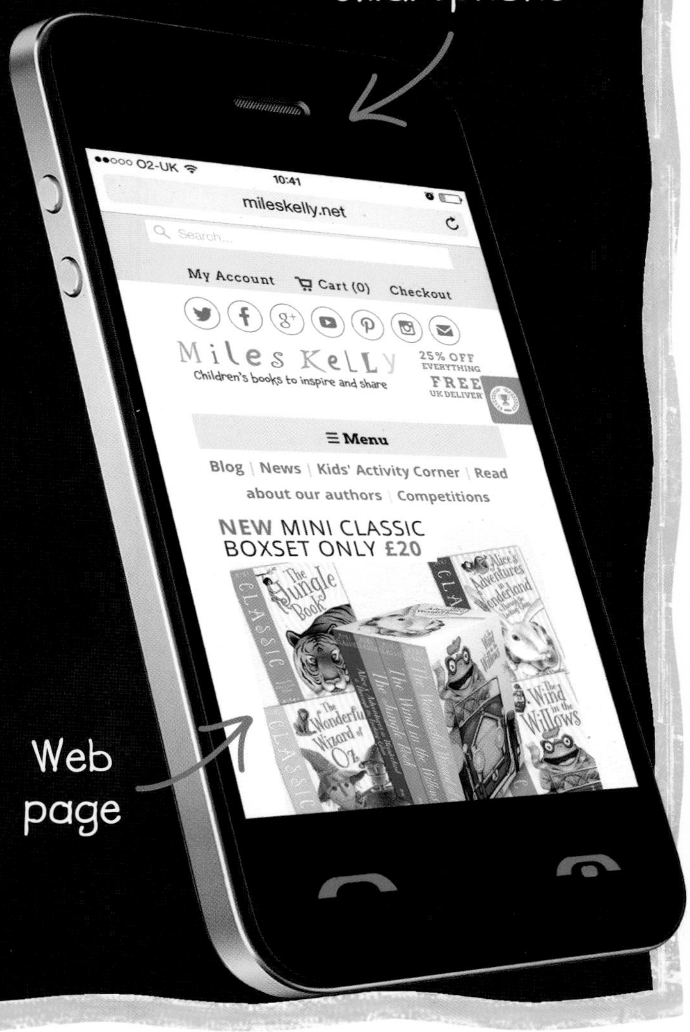

Plenty of pages

The World Wide Web has more than 8000 million pages of information. That's two pages for every person on the planet!

can a car be made from card?

Think

Can you think of other materials from which things are made? If you get stuck, ask a grown-up.

Yes, it can – but it would break if you sat inside it! It is always important to use the right material to make something. Cars are made from tough, long-lasting materials, like metal, plastic and rubber.

A racing car is made up of hundreds of parts and different materials

Cotton plants make clothes

What materials grow?

Many of the materials we use every day come from plants. Wood comes from the trunks and branches of trees. Cotton is made from the seeds of cotton plants to make clothes such as T-shirts. Some rubber is made from a liquid (sap) from rubber trees.

Rubber trees make tyres

Tree trunks and branches make wooden bats

Does glass grow?

Glass doesn't grow. It is made from sand and two other materials called limestone and soda. These materials are mixed together and melted to make a gooey liquid. When the mixture cools down, it forms the hard glass that we use to make windows, drinking glasses and other objects.

Bullet proof

Some glass is extra-strong. Toughened glass is so hard that even a bullet from a gun bounces off it!

what do scientists do at work?

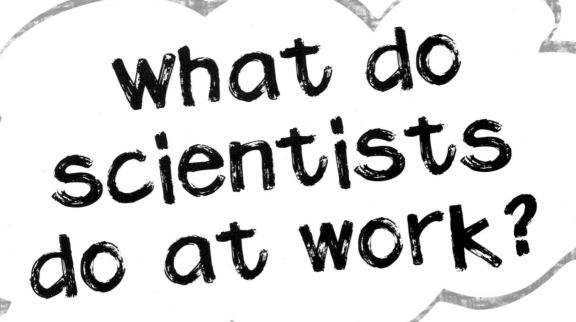

Some scientists try to find out about the world around us. Others find out about space, planets and stars. Some scientists discover useful materials that we can use.

Scientists carry out experiments in laboratories to test their ideas.

Scientists in a laboratory

Albert Einstein

Who is the most famous scientist?

The most famous scientist is called Albert Einstein (1879–1955). He made many discoveries about time, space, the force of gravity and nuclear energy. The ideas that Einstein wrote down were so amazing that they made him famous across the world.

Find

Where was Albert Einstein born? Can you find out? Use an encyclopedia or the Internet to help you.

Atom pie

One hundred years ago, scientists thought that the tiny pieces in an atom were all spread out, like raisins in a pudding. Now we know they are all bunched together.

Do scientists help doctors?

Yes, they do. Many scientists make medicines that the doctor gives you when you are ill. They also help to make the complicated machines that doctors use in hospitals. Scientists also try to find out what makes us ill, and how we can stay healthy.

Are animals part of science?

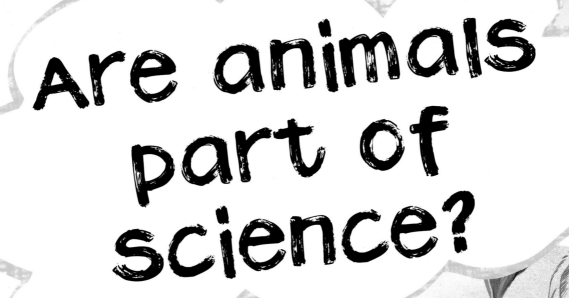

Yes, they are. Scientists who study animals and plants work everywhere in the world. They study in hot rainforests, dusty deserts, high mountains, at the freezing poles and in rivers and seas.

Ecologists study animals and plants

LOOK

Study the picture. Can you see something that might harm the animals and plants?

Which way?

Some animals travel great distances around the world. They use the Earth's magnetic field to guide them.

What is an ecologist?

An ecologist is a scientist. Ecologists study where plants and animals live. They also look at how plants and animals live alongside each other, and the things that animals eat. Ecologists also study the harm that we do to animals.

How do ecologists follow animals?

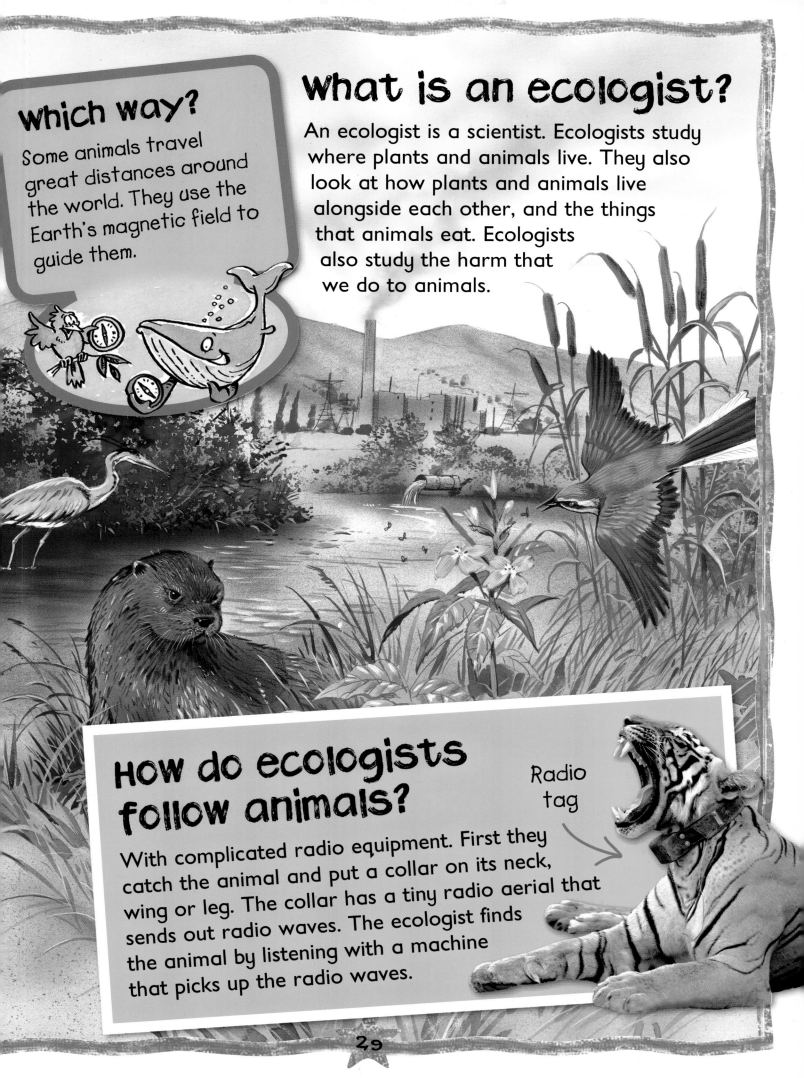

With complicated radio equipment. First they catch the animal and put a collar on its neck, wing or leg. The collar has a tiny radio aerial that sends out radio waves. The ecologist finds the animal by listening with a machine that picks up the radio waves.

Are we harming the Earth?

Many of the things we do are harming the world around us. Machines such as cars put dangerous gases into the air. These gases can harm plants and make people ill. They are also making the weather change. Scientists are looking for new ways to reduce damage to the Earth.

Dirty cars

Cars and other vehicles can produce so much pollution that in some cities it has become difficult for people to breathe.

What is recycling?

Recycling is using materials again, instead of throwing them away. This helps to make less waste and reduces the use of raw materials. Glass, paper, metal and plastic can all be recycled and turned into new products.

Recycling

Does electricity harm the Earth?

Yes, it does. Lots of coal, oil and gas are burned to make electricity. These make harmful gases that go into the air. You can help by turning things off to save electricity. Scientists are inventing new ways of making electricity from the wind, the Sun and water.

Save

Ask your family to save electricity. Get them to switch off the lights when nobody is in the room.

Quiz time

Do you remember what you have read about science? These questions will test your memory. The pictures will help you. If you get stuck, read the pages again.

1. Is science in the playground?

page 6

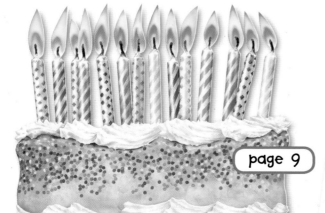

2. How do candles burn?

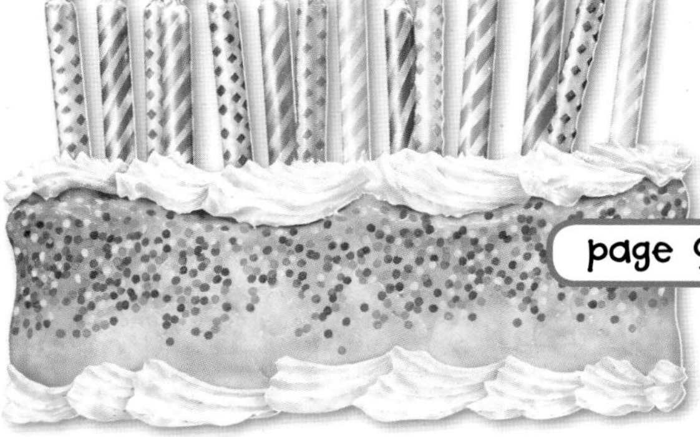

page 9

3. What is a thermometer?

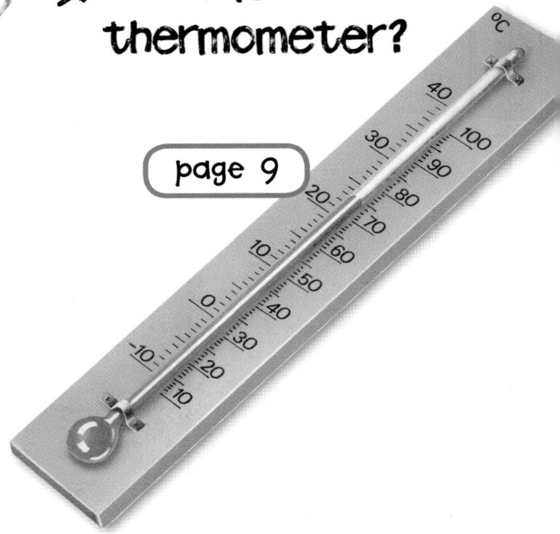

page 9

4. What is inside an electric motor?

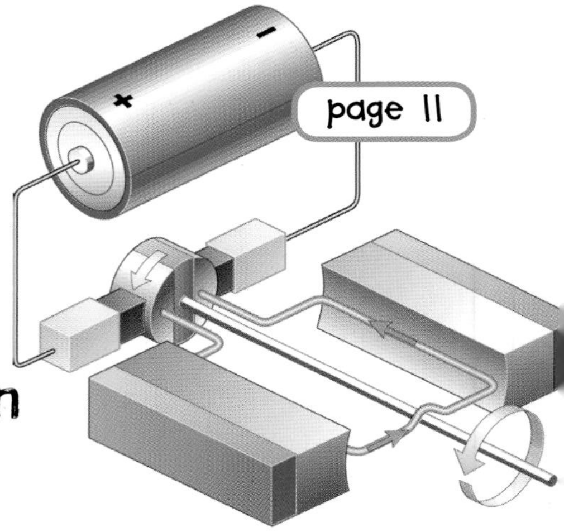

page 11

5. How do skyscrapers stay up?

page 13

6. Does a magnet have a field?

page 15

7. What are poles?

page 15

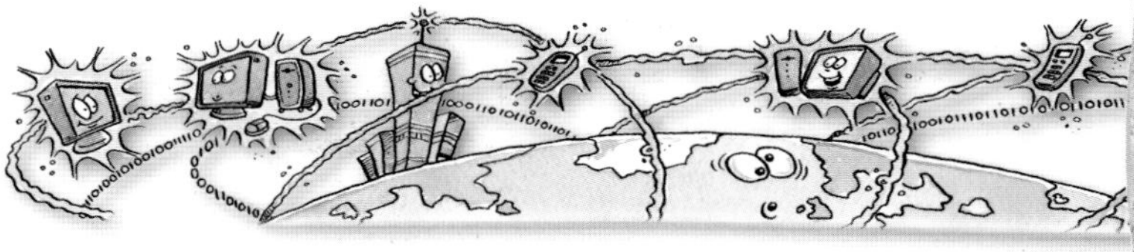

page 22

11. What does www stand for?

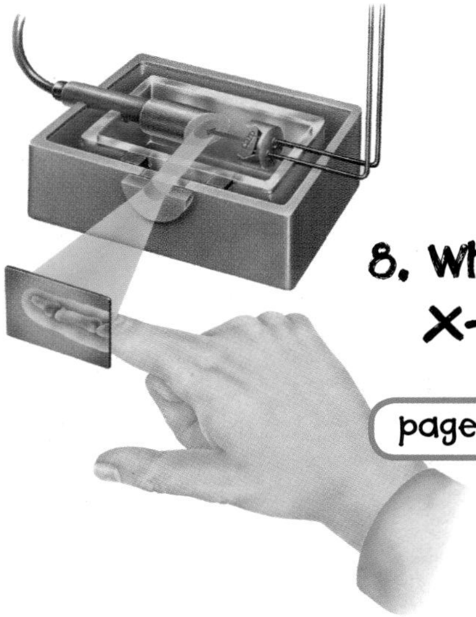

8. What is an X-ray?

page 19

12. Who is the most famous scientist?

page 27

13. Does electricity harm the Earth?

page 31

page 20

9. Are computers clever?

page 21

10. Does a computer have a brain?

Answers

1. Yes it is, in rides such as see-saws
2. By melting wax, which becomes a vapour that burns
3. Something that measures heat
4. Magnets and wires
5. They have a strong frame that supports them
6. Yes, a magnetic field
7. Poles are where the pull of a magnet is strongest
8. It is like a radio wave
9. Not really, but they can carry out complicated programs of instruction
10. It has an electronic brain
11. World Wide Web
12. Albert Einstein
13. Yes, it can

Human Body

Why do babies grip so tightly?

Tiny babies can do simple things. If something touches a baby's cheek, it turns its head and tries to suck. If something touches the baby's hand, it grips tightly. These actions are called reflexes. They help the baby survive.

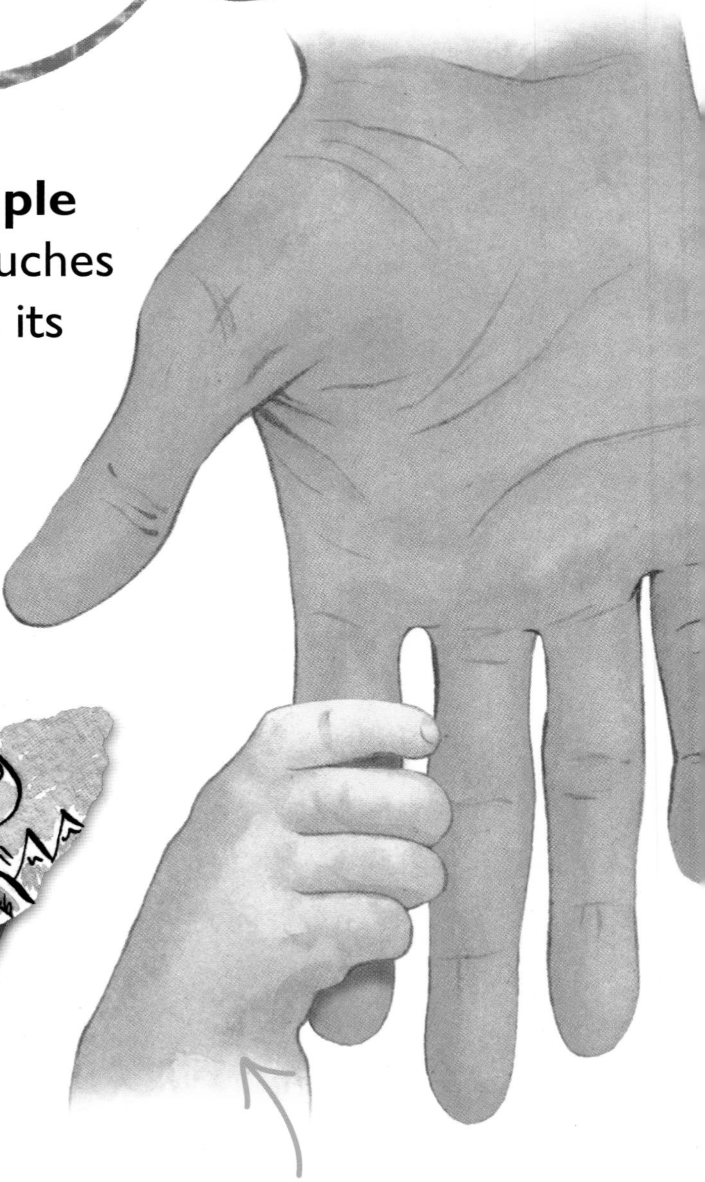

Baby gripping

Giant baby

A baby grows quickly before it is born. If it grew this fast for 50 years, it would be taller than Mount Everest!

When do babies start to walk?

Usually when they are about one year old. Babies can roll over at three months. At six months, they can sit up. At nine months they start to crawl. Then babies learn to stand and take their first steps.

Find out

Why do you think a newborn baby cries? Ask a grown-up if you need any help.

Am I always learning?

Yes, you are! Most children start school when they are five years old. They learn to count, read, write and draw. Children learn outside of the classroom, too. Playing and having fun with friends is a great way to learn new things!

Children playing

What does my skin do?

Skin protects you from bumps and scratches. It stops your body from drying out, and prevents germs from getting in. When you play on bikes or skateboards, you should wear gloves and knee pads to protect your skin.

Gloves protect from scrapes
Knee pads protect from cuts

Ouch! Ouch! Ouch!

There are millions of tiny touch sensors in your skin. They tell your brain when something touches your skin. Some sensors feel hot and cold. Others feel pain. Ouch!

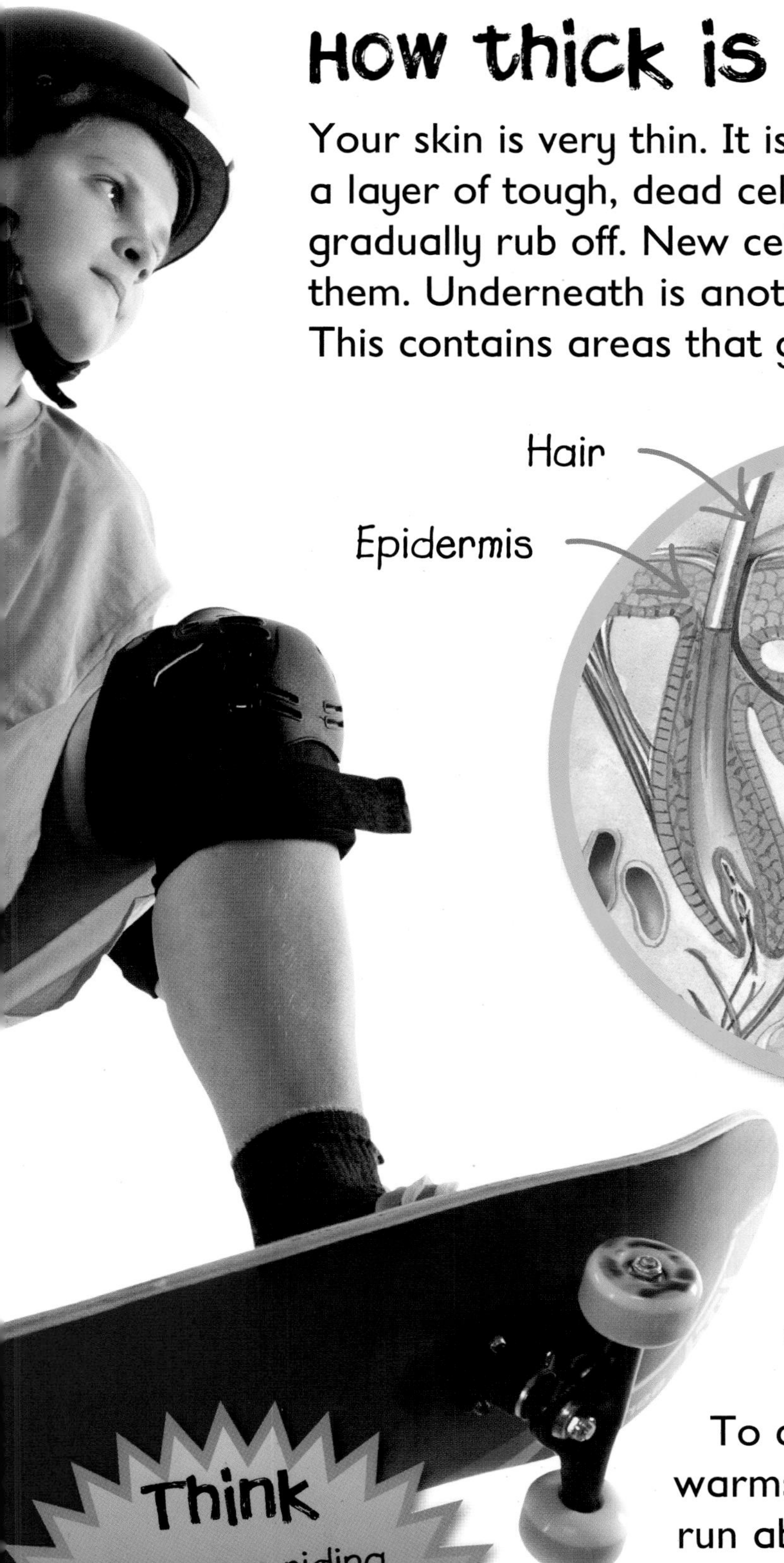

How thick is my skin?

Your skin is very thin. It is only 2 millimetres thick. On top is a layer of tough, dead cells called the epidermis. These cells gradually rub off. New cells grow underneath to replace them. Underneath is another layer of skin called the dermis. This contains areas that give you your sense of touch.

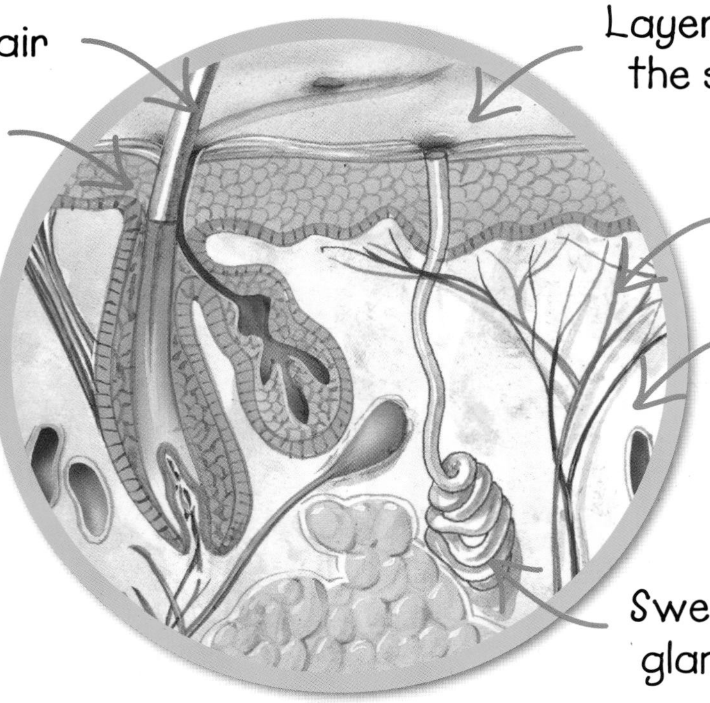

Why do I sweat when I'm warm?

To cool down again. Your body warms up on a hot day or when you run about. You sweat to get rid of the heat. Your body lets sweat out through your skin. As the sweat dries, it takes away heat. This cools you down.

Think

If you are riding a bike or playing on a skateboard, what should you wear on your head, and why?

How much hair do I have?

Your whole body is covered in about five million hairs! You have about 100,000 hairs on your head. Hair grows out of tiny pits in your skin, called follicles. It grows in different colours and can be wavy, curly or straight.

What are nails made from?

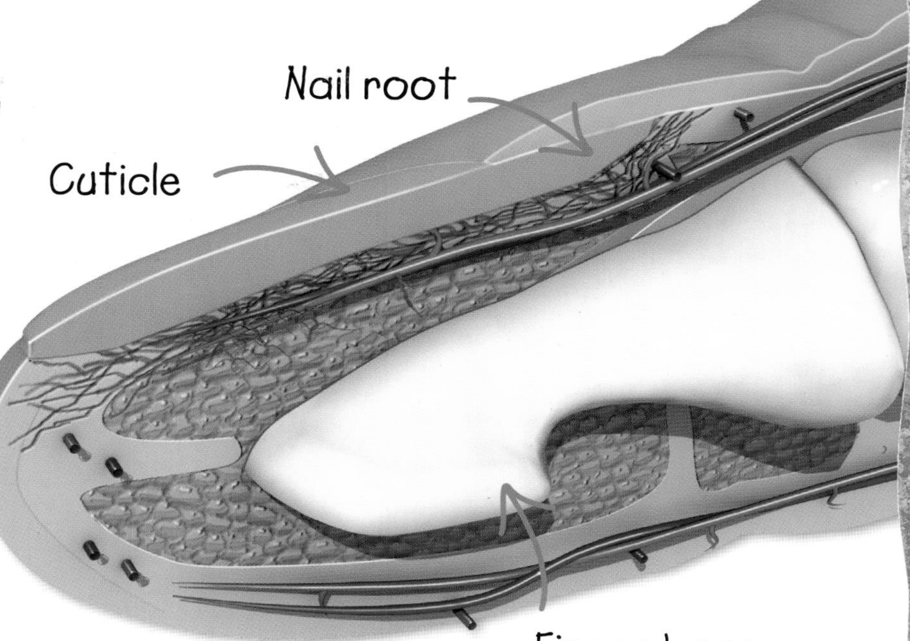

Fingernails and toenails are made from a hard material called keratin. This is the same material that hair is made from. Nails grow out of the nail root. In a week, a nail grows about half a millimetre. They grow faster at night than in the day!

For the chop

The hair on your head grows about 2 millimetres a week. If a hair is never cut, it reaches about one metre in length before falling out. It is replaced by a new hair.

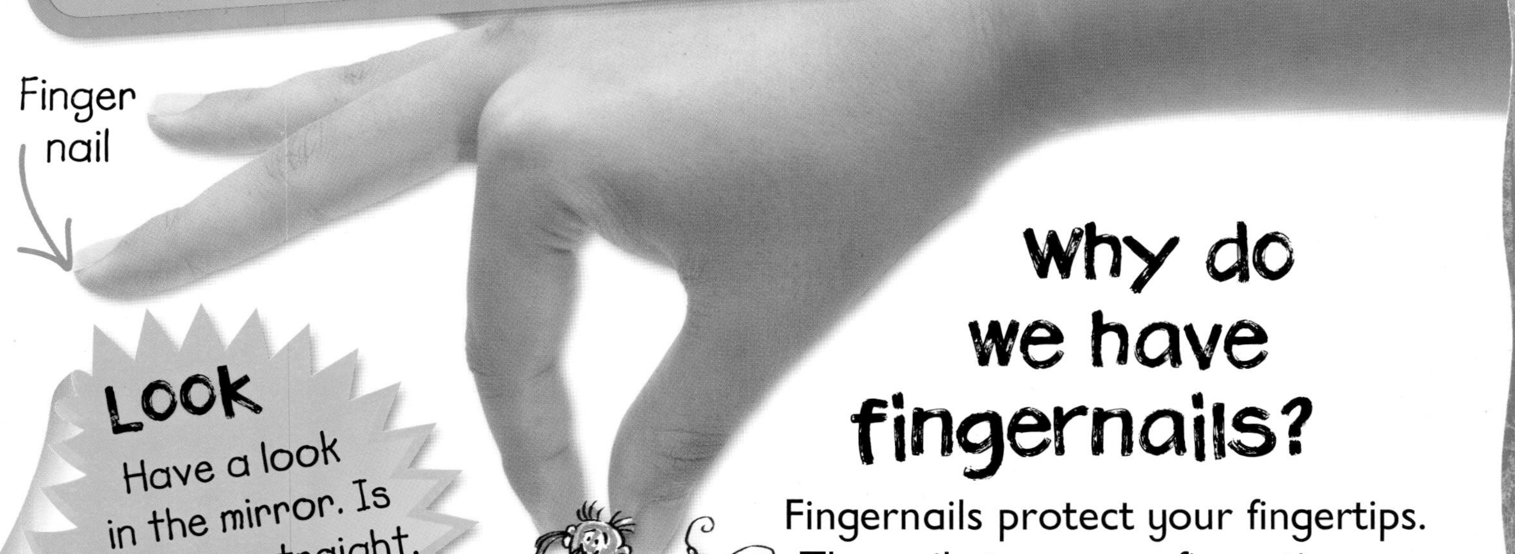

Look

Have a look in the mirror. Is your hair straight, wavy or curly? Use the pictures on page 40 to help you.

Why do we have fingernails?

Fingernails protect your fingertips. The nail stops your fingertip bending back when you touch something. This helps your fingers to feel things. Nails are useful for picking up tiny objects.

How many bones do I have?

Most people have 206 bones. Half of them are in your hands and feet. All your bones together make up your skeleton. The skeleton is like a frame. It holds up the other parts of your body. It also protects the squashy bits inside.

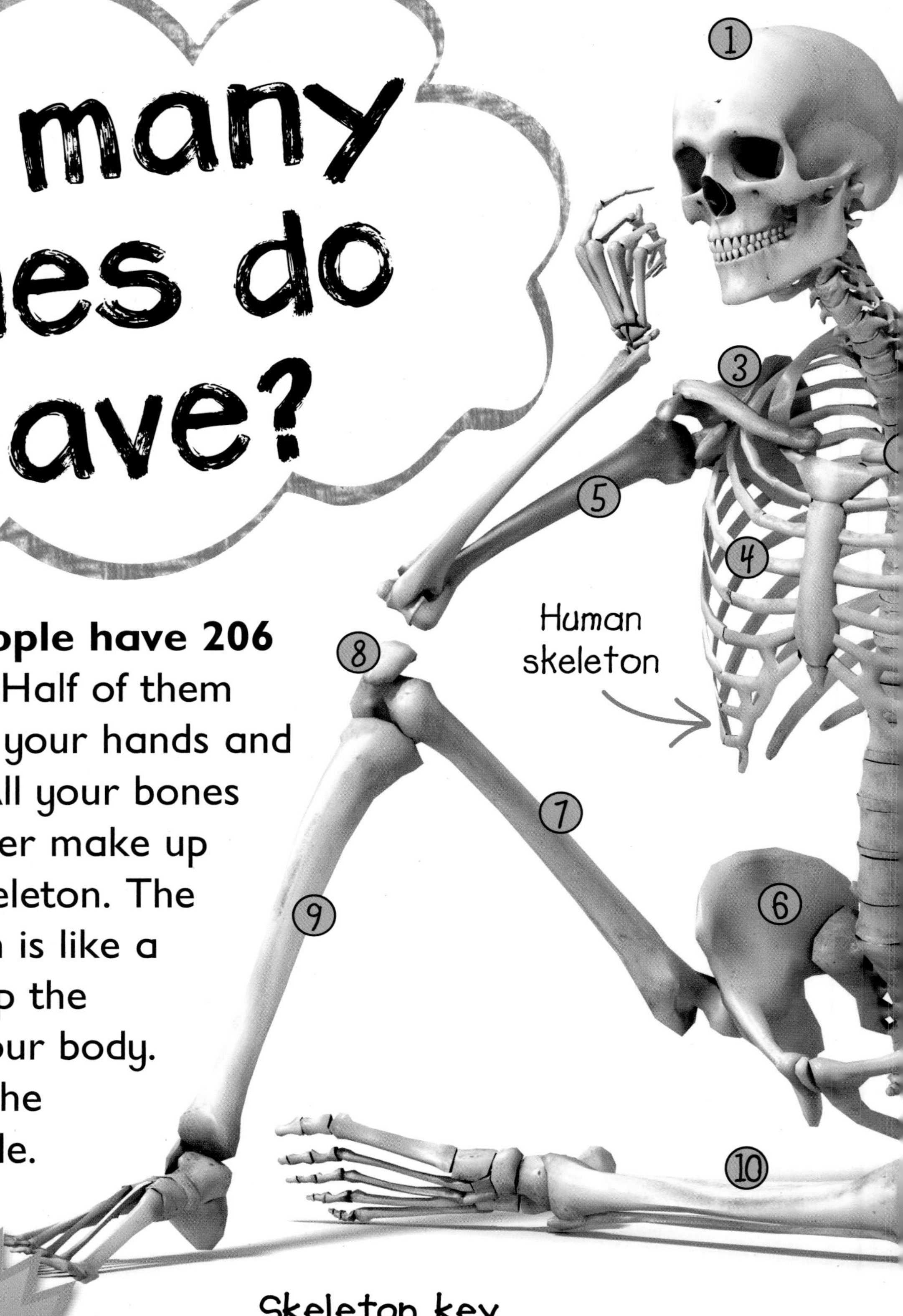

Find

Can you find your collarbone? It starts at your shoulder and runs to the top of your rib cage.

Skeleton key

1. Skull
2. Collar bone
3. Shoulder blade
4. Ribs
5. Upper arm bone
6. Pelvis
7. Thigh bone
8. Kneecap
9. Calf bone
10. Shin bone

Strong bones

Your bone is lightweight but super-strong. It is stronger than concrete or steel, which are used for making buildings and bridges! But bones can still break if they are bent too much.

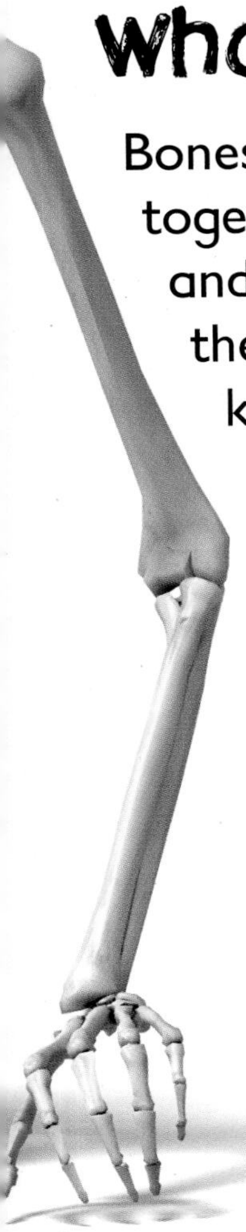

What are bones made from?

Bones are made from different materials mixed together. Some of the materials are very hard and some are tough and bendy. Together they make bones very strong. There is a kind of jelly called marrow inside some bones. This makes tiny parts for your blood, called red and white cells.

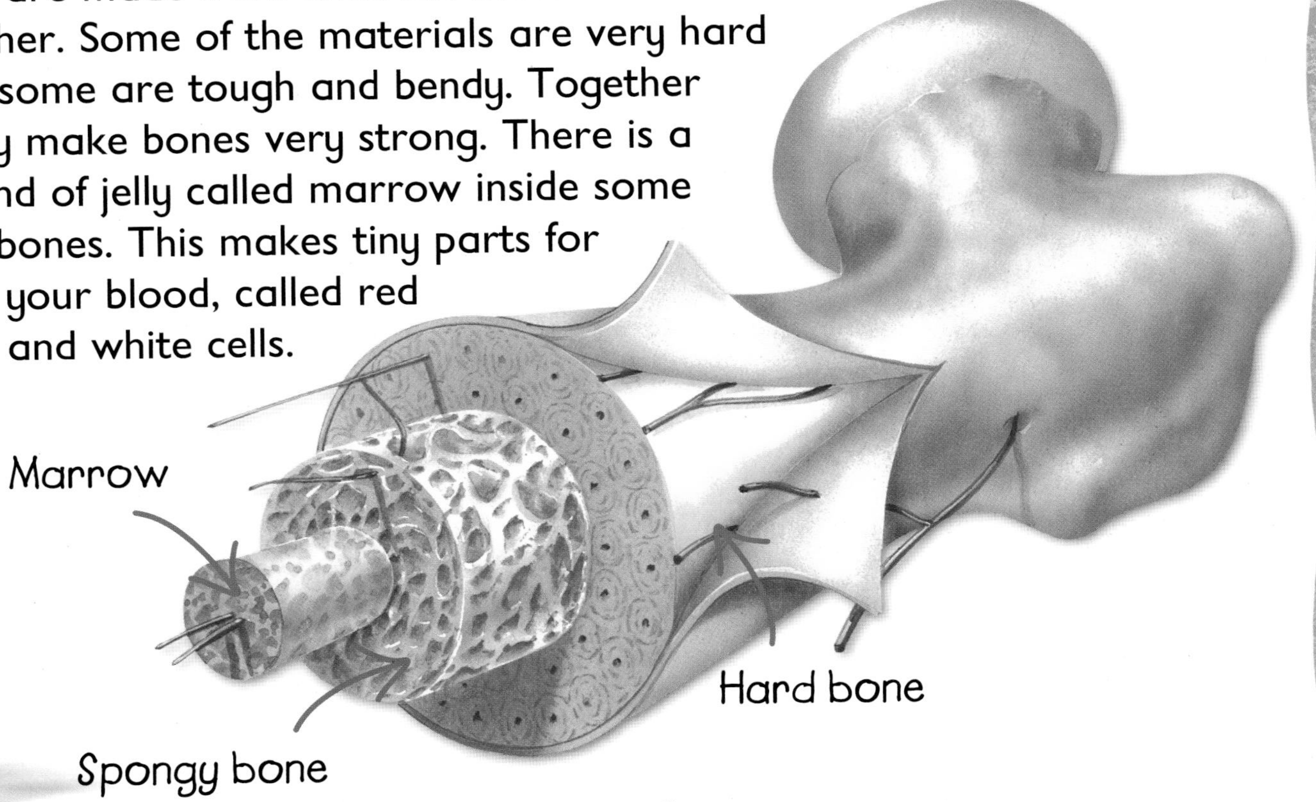

How are bones joined together?

Your bones are connected by joints. They let your back, arms, legs, fingers and toes move. You have about 100 joints in your body. The largest of your joints are in your hips and knees. The smallest joints are inside your ear.

How do muscles work?

Muscles are made from fibres that look like bits of string. The fibres get shorter to make the muscle pull. The biggest muscles in your body are in your bottom! You use them when you walk and run. The strongest muscle in your body is in your jaw.

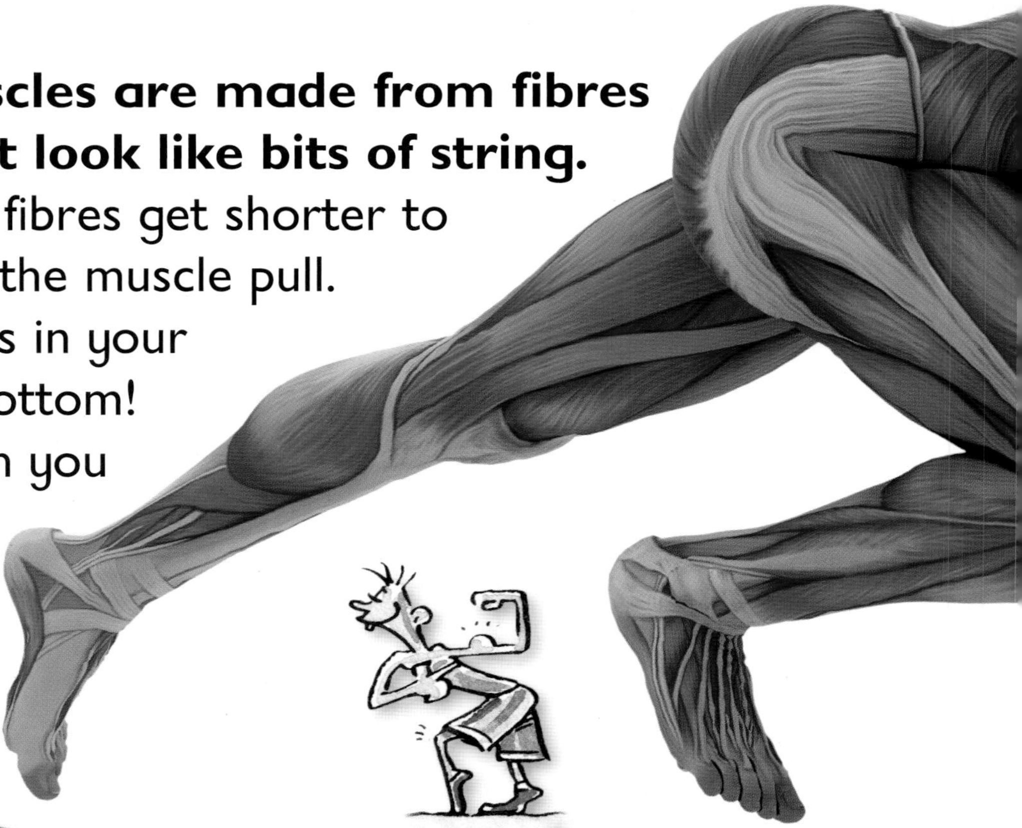

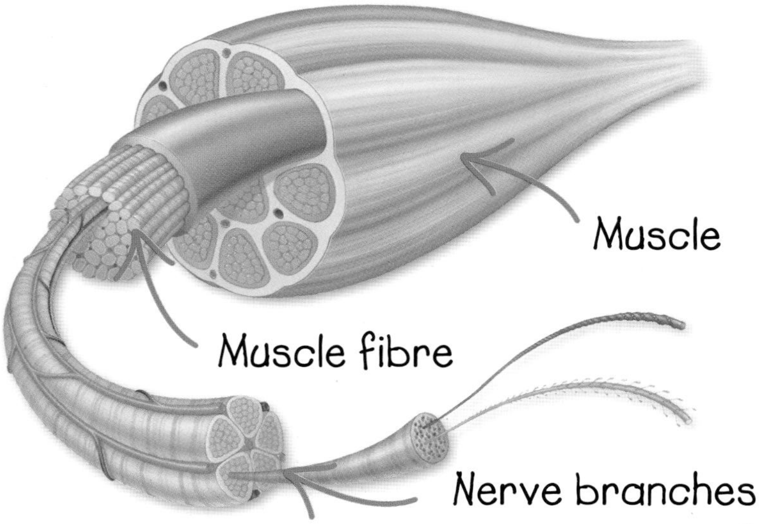

How do joints bend?

Muscles make your joints, such as your elbows and knees, bend. They help you to run, jump, hold and lift things. In fact you need muscles to move all of your body.

Cheeky muscles

Your face is full of muscles. You use them to smile, to wrinkle your nose, or to cry. You use more muscles to frown than to smile!

What makes my muscles move?

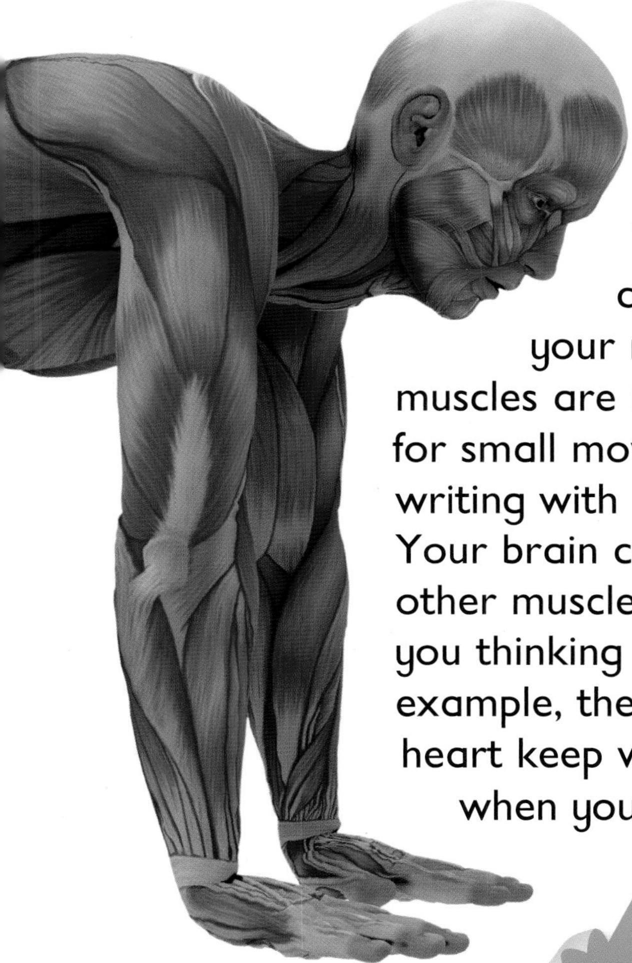

Your brain does. It sends messages along nerves to your muscles. Lots of muscles are needed, even for small movements, like writing with a pen. Your brain controls other muscles without you thinking about it. For example, the muscles in your heart keep working even when you are asleep.

Human muscular skeleton

Feel

Bend and unbend your arm. Can you feel your arm muscles getting shorter and longer?

Why do I need to breathe?

You breathe to take air into your body. There is a gas in the air called oxygen that your body needs to work. The air goes up your nose or into your mouth. Then it goes down a tube called the windpipe and into your lungs.

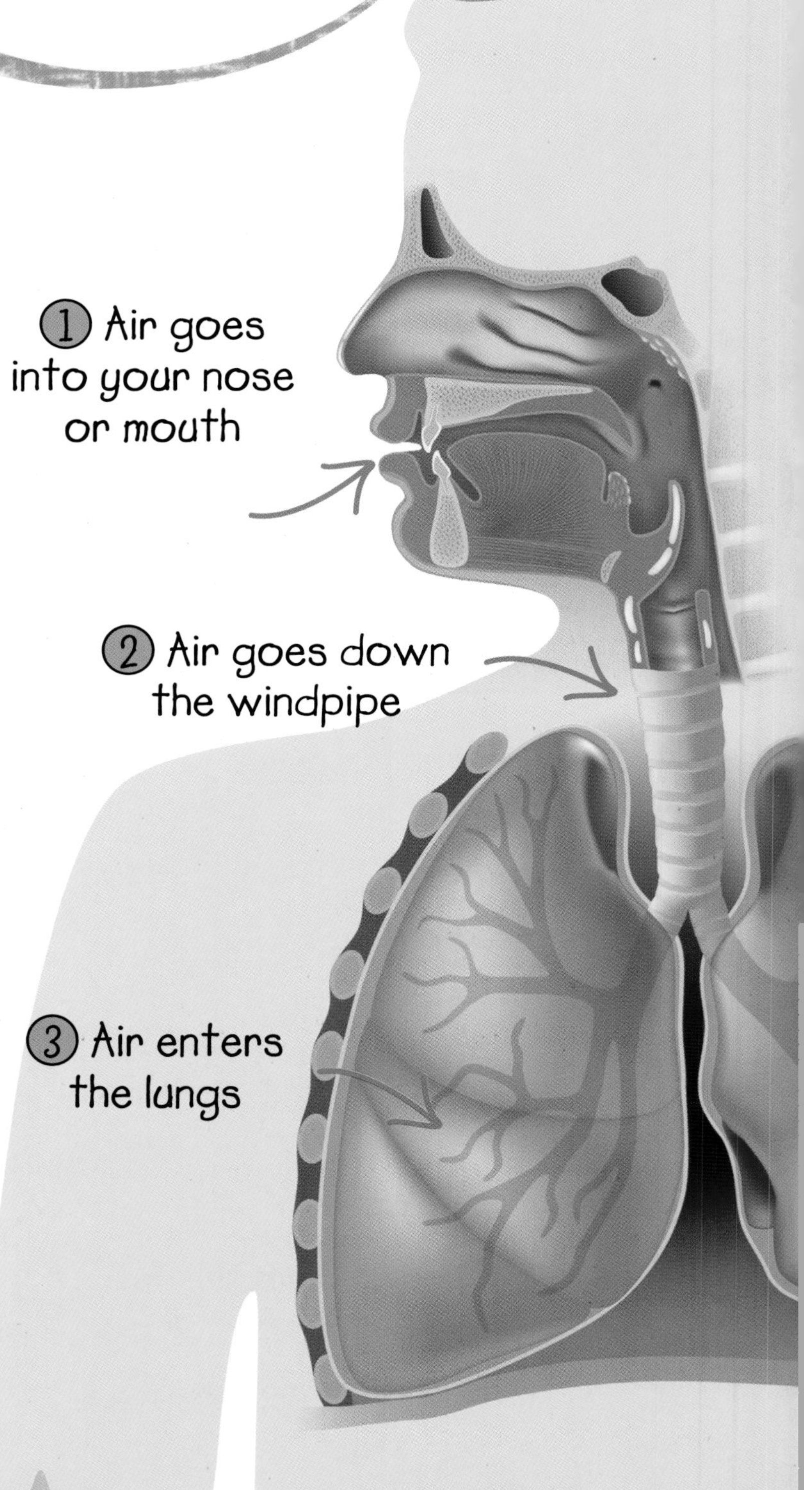

1 Air goes into your nose or mouth
2 Air goes down the windpipe
3 Air enters the lungs

Count

How many times do you breathe in and out in one minute?

Is my voice kept in a box?

Not quite! The real name for your voicebox is the larynx. It's at the top of the windpipe, and makes a bulge at the front of your neck. Air passing through the voicebox makes it shake, or vibrate. This is the sound of your voice. Your voice can make lots of sounds, and helps you to sing!

Fill 'em up

When you are resting, you take in enough air to fill a can of fizzy drink in every breath. When you are running, you breathe in ten times as much air.

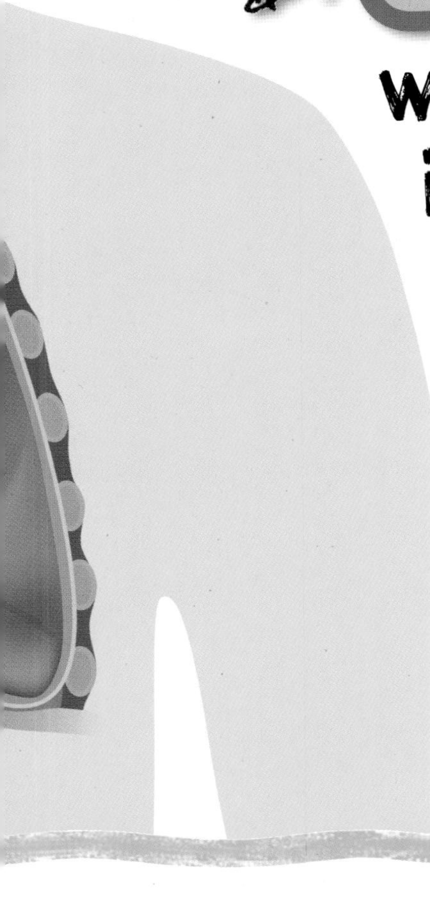

What makes air go into my lungs?

There is a big muscle under your lungs that moves down. More muscles make your ribs move out, making your lungs bigger. Air rushes into your lungs to fill the space and when your muscles relax, the air is pushed out again.

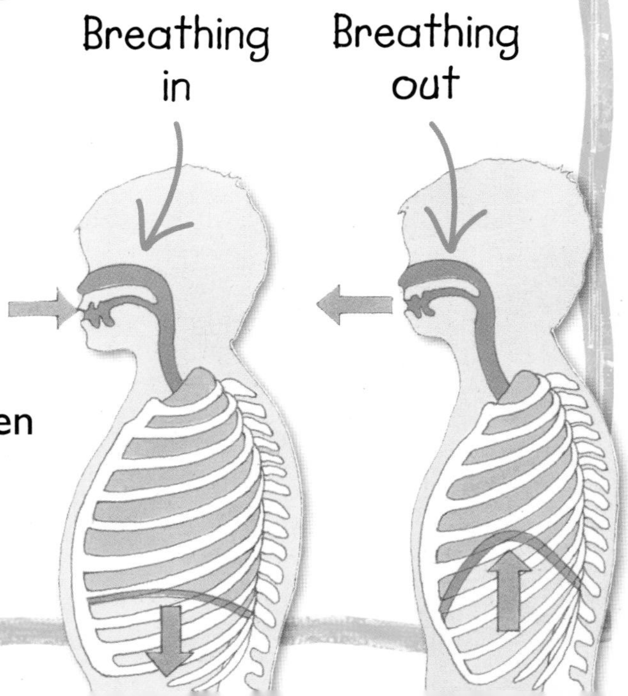

What food is good for me?

Lots of food is good for you! Different foods give your body the goodness it needs. Fruit and vegetables are very good for you. Bread and pasta give you energy. Small amounts of fat, such as cheese, keep your nerves healthy. Chicken and fish keep your muscles strong.

Bread gives energy
Fruit is full of goodness
Vegetables help digestion

Eating elephants

You eat about one kilogram of food every day. During your life, you will eat about 30 tonnes of food. That's the same weight as six elephants!

Draw

Look at the pictures on these pages. Can you draw a healthy meal that you would like to eat?

What happens when I swallow?

The first thing you do with food is chew it, then you swallow lumps of the chewed food. As you do this, the food goes down a tube called the oesophagus (gullet). Muscles in the oesophagus push the food into your stomach.

Fats keep nerves healthy

Fish helps muscles to grow strong

Sugars are needed in small quantities

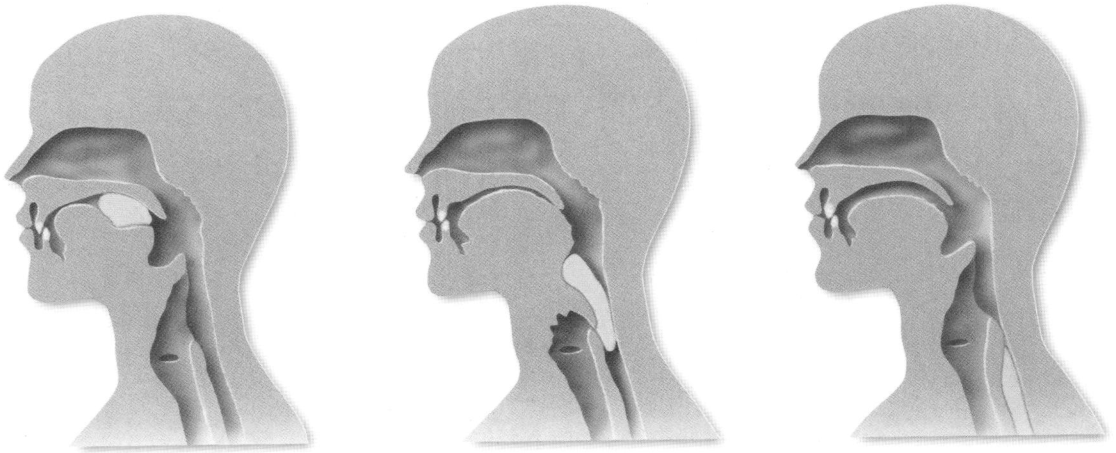

1. Tongue pushes food to the back of the throat
2. Throat muscles squeeze the food downwards
3. The oesophagus pushes food to the stomach

Why do I need to eat food?

Food keeps your body working. It is like fuel for your body. It keeps your body going through the day and night, and works your muscles. Food also contains things your body needs to grow, repair itself and fight illness.

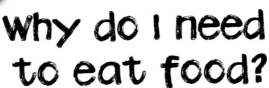

What are teeth made of?

Teeth are covered in a material called enamel. This is harder than most kinds of rock! Teeth are fixed into your jaw bones by roots. Sharp front teeth (incisors) bite food into small pieces. Tall, pointy teeth (canines) tear and pull food. Flat back teeth (molars) chew food to a mush.

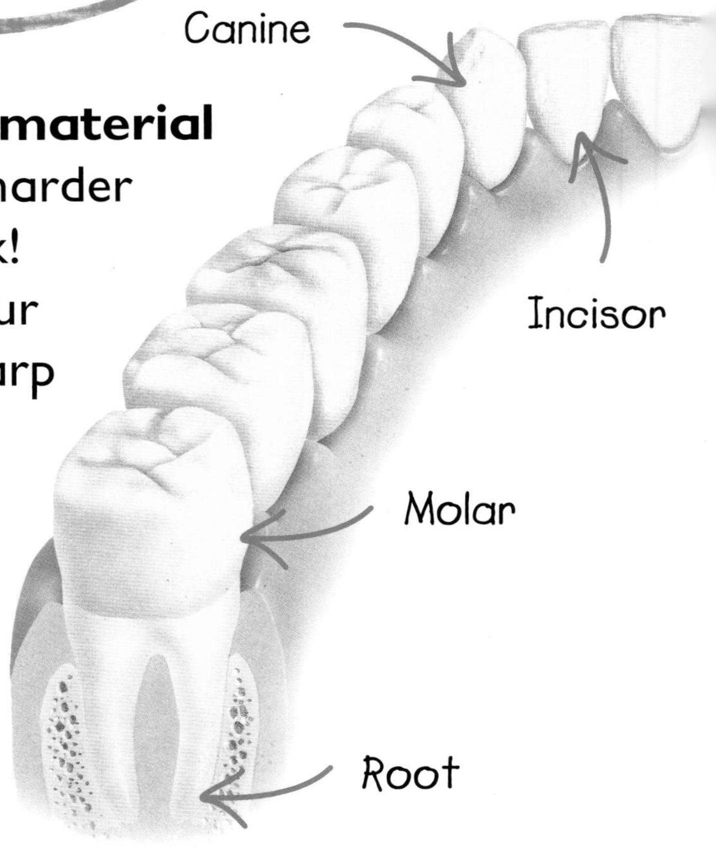

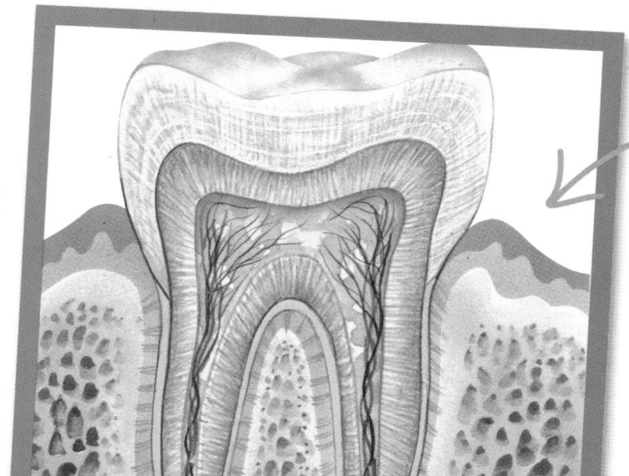

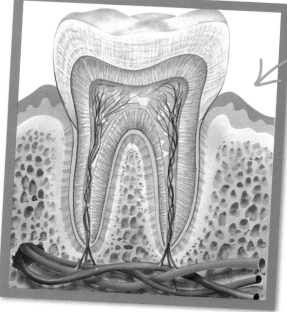

How many sets of teeth do I have?

You have two sets. A baby is born without teeth. The first set of teeth appears when a child is six months old. This set has 20 teeth. These teeth usually start to fall out at about seven years old, and are replaced by 32 adult teeth.

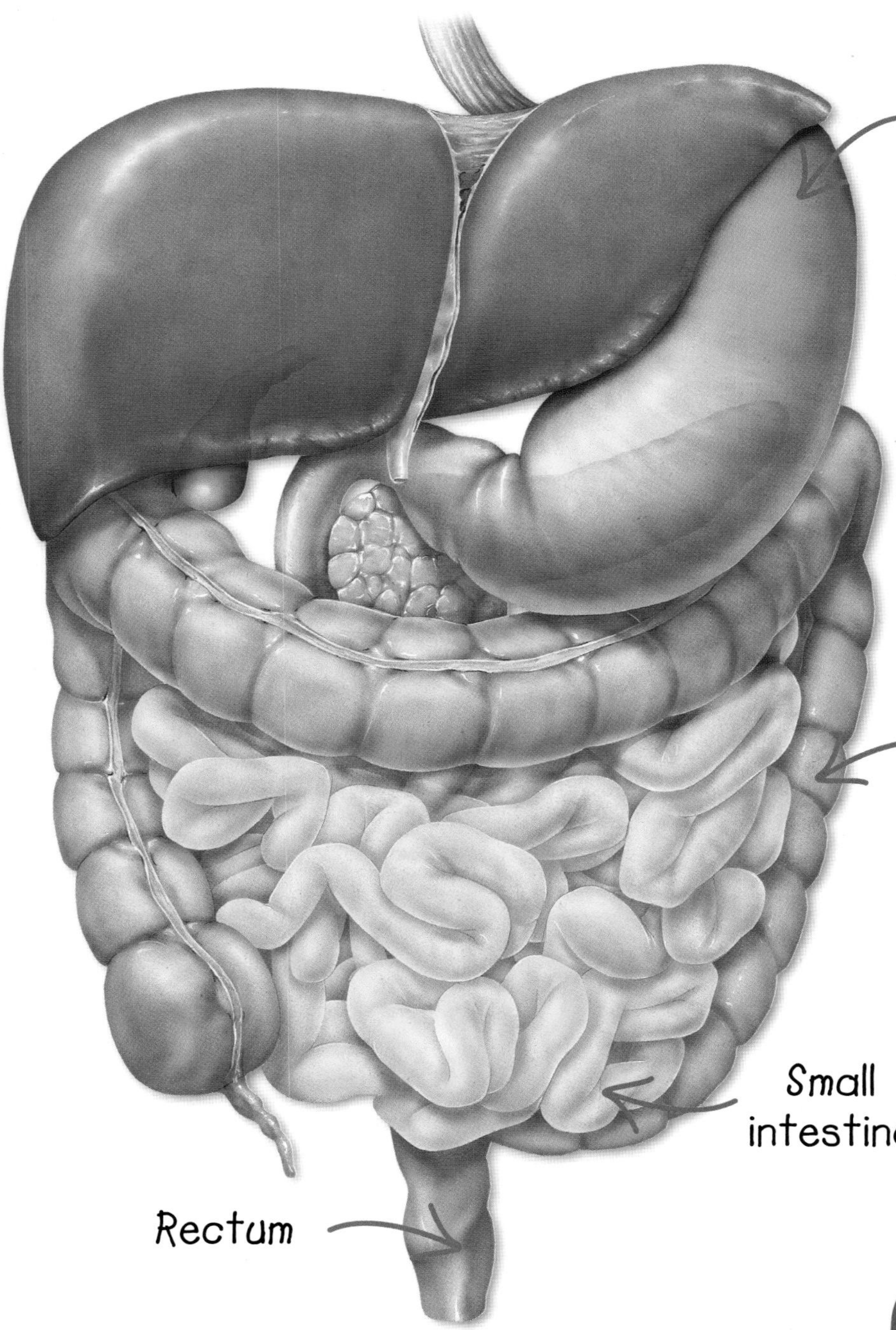

Discover

Do you still have your first set of teeth, or have your baby teeth begun to fall out?

What happens to the food I swallow?

The food you swallow goes into your stomach. Here, special juices and strong muscles break the food up into a thick mush. The mushy food then goes into a long tube called the intestines. Here, all the goodness from the food is taken out, to be used by our body.

All gone

When you go to the toilet, you get rid of waste. This is leftover food. It is stored in your large intestine until you go to the toilet.

Why does my heart beat?

To pump blood and oxygen around your body. Your heart is about the size of your fist and is made of muscle. When it beats, your heart squeezes blood into tubes. These tubes carry blood and oxygen around your body. The blood then comes back to the heart from the lungs, with more oxygen.

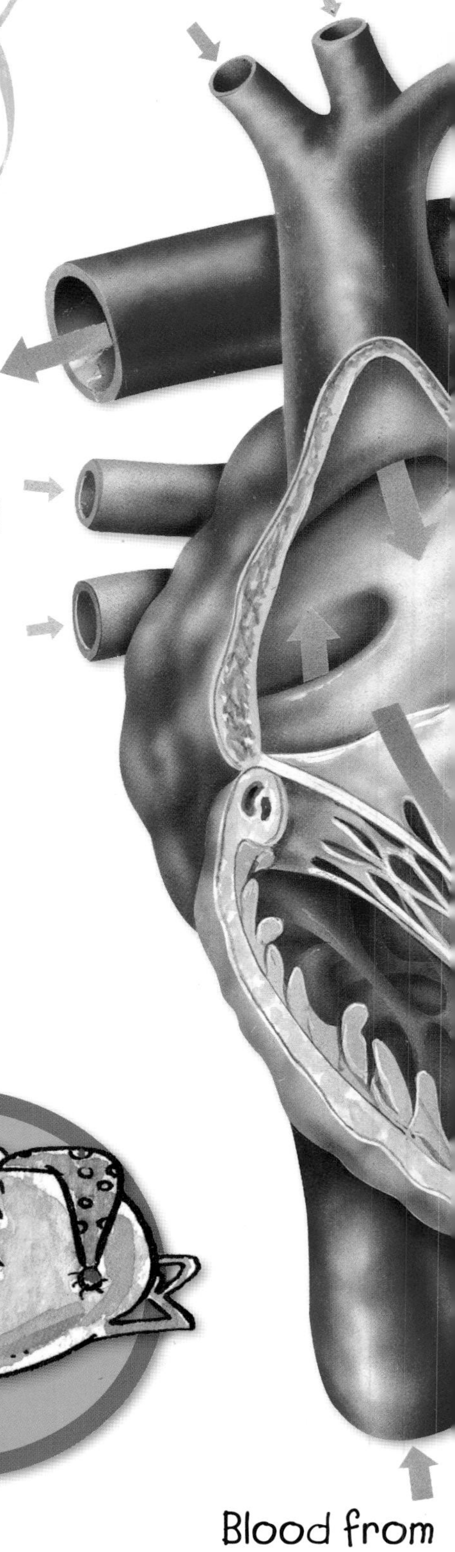

Beat of life

Your heart beats once a second for the whole of your life. That is 86,000 beats a day, and 31 million beats a year. In total, this is 2000 million beats in your life.

What does blood do?

Your whole body needs oxygen to work. Blood carries oxygen to every part of your body in its red cells. Blood also contains white cells that fight germs. Tubes called arteries and veins carry blood around your body.

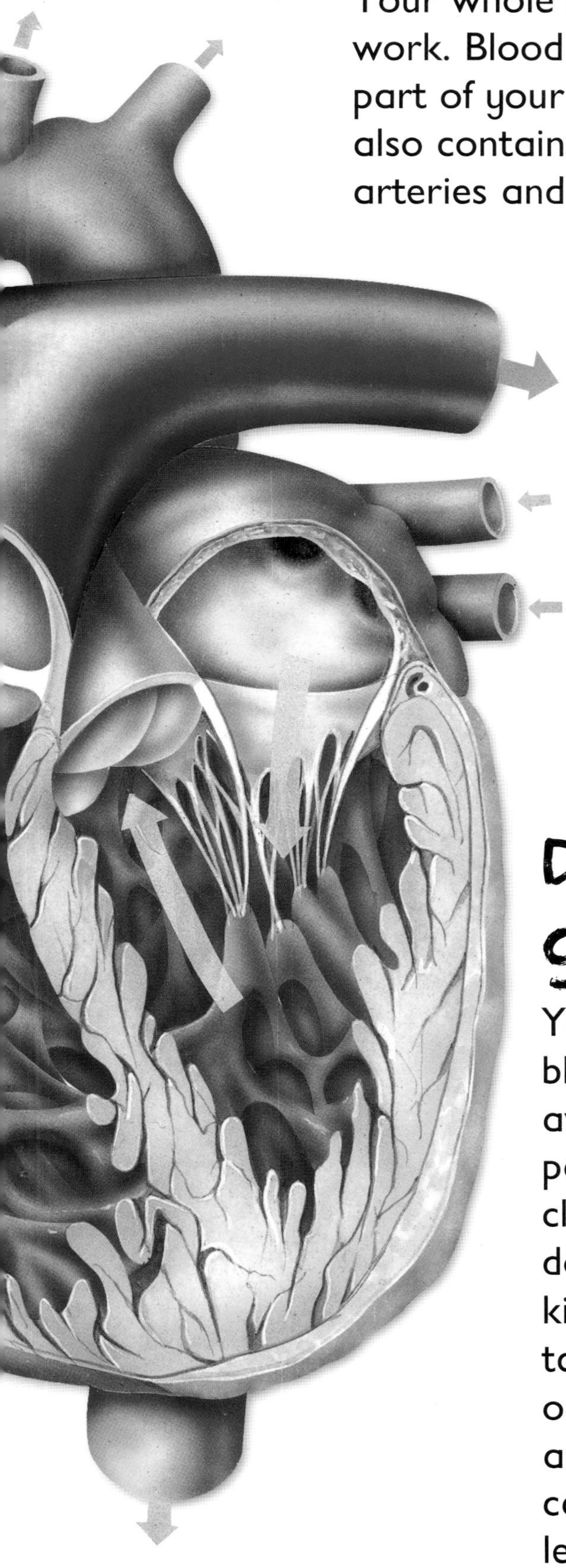

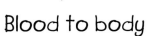

Feel

Touch your neck under your chin. Can you feel the blood flowing through an artery to your brain?

Does blood get dirty?

Yes, it does. Because blood carries waste away from your body parts, it has to be cleaned. This is done by your kidneys. They take the waste out of the blood and make a liquid called urine. This liquid leaves your body when you go to the toilet.

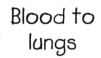

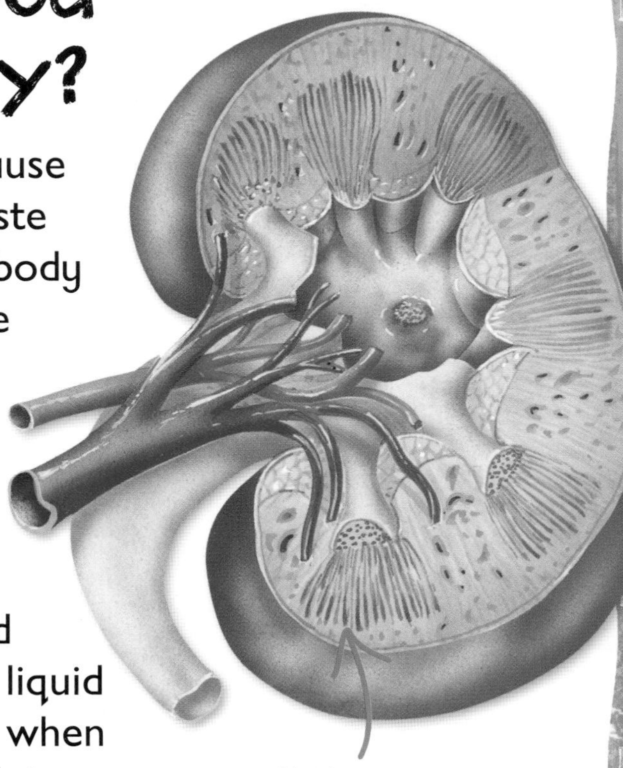

Are my eyes like a camera?

Your eyes work like a tiny camera. They collect light that bounces off the things you are looking at. This makes tiny pictures at the back of the eyes. Here, millions of sensors pick up the light. They send a picture to your brain along a nerve.

Look

Look in the mirror at your eye. Can you see the dark pupil where light goes in?

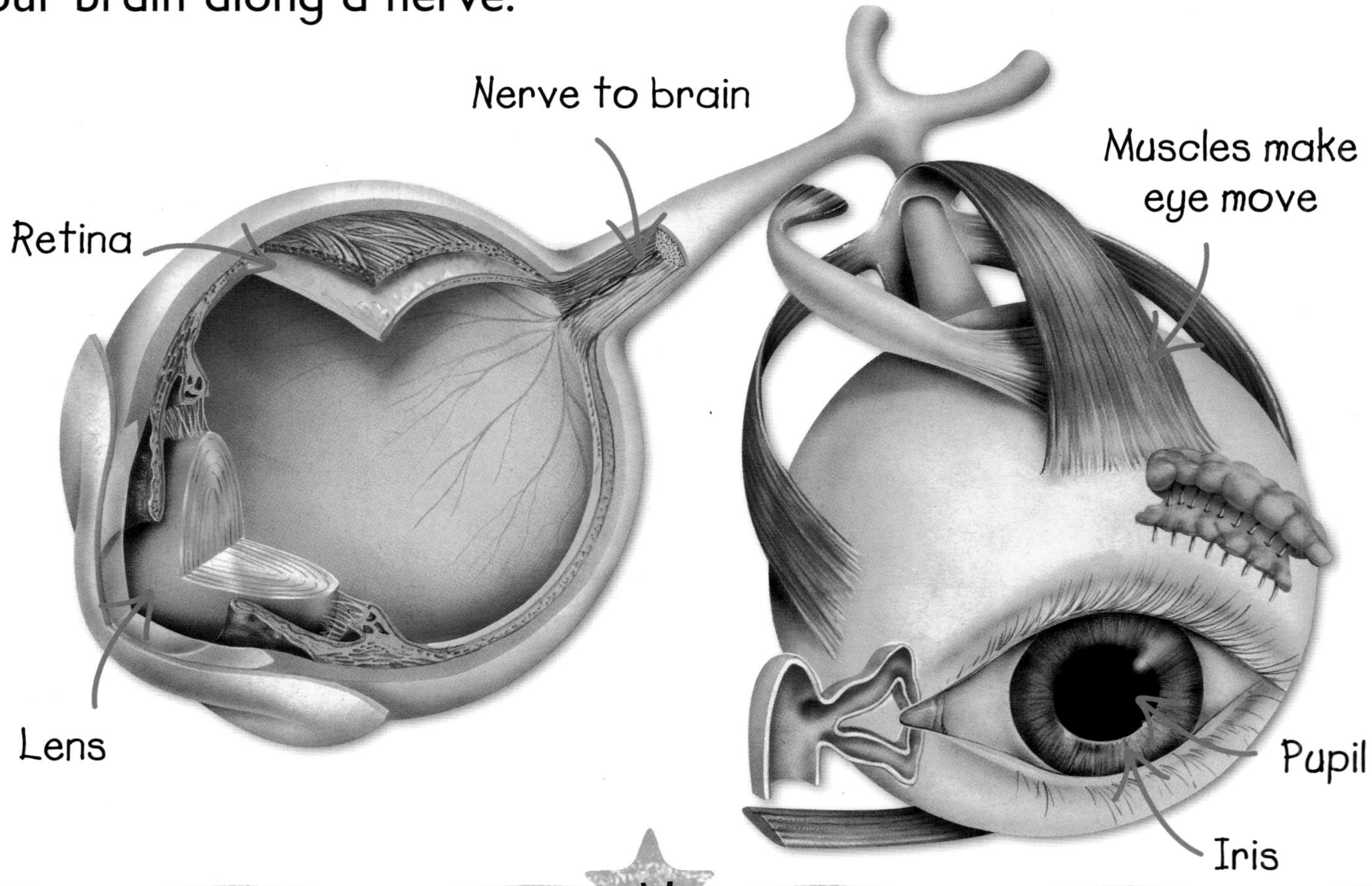

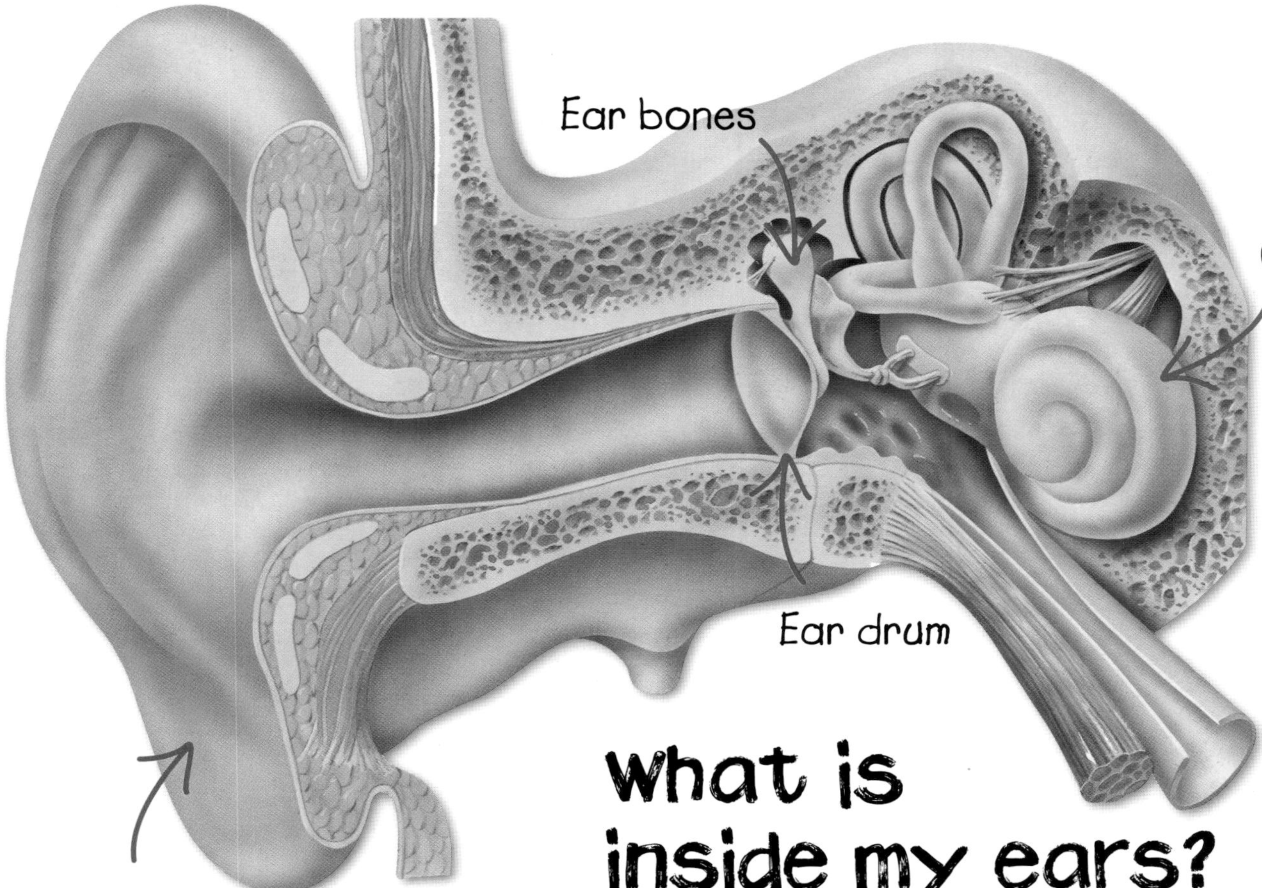

What is inside my ears?

The flap on your head is only part of your ear. The hole in your ear goes to a tiny piece of tight skin, called an eardrum. Sounds enter your ear and make the eardrum move in and out. Tiny bones pass these movements to the cochlea, which is shaped like a snail. This is filled with liquid.

How do I hear sounds?

The cochlea in your ear contains thousands of tiny hairs. It is also full of liquid. Sounds make the liquid move. This makes the hairs wave about. Tiny sensors pick up the waving, and send messages to your brain so you hear the sound.

In a spin

Inside your ear are loops full of liquid. They can tell if you move your head. This helps you to balance. If you spin around, the fluid keeps moving. This makes you feel dizzy!

Why can't I see smells?

Because they're invisible! Smells are tiny particles that float in the air. Inside the top of your nose are sticky smell sensors. When you sniff something, the sensors collect the smell particles. They send messages to your brain, which tell you what you can smell.

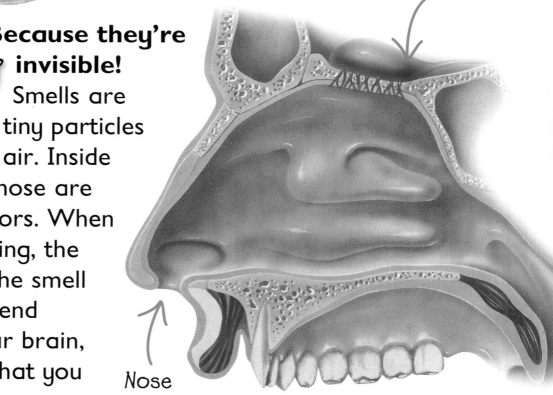

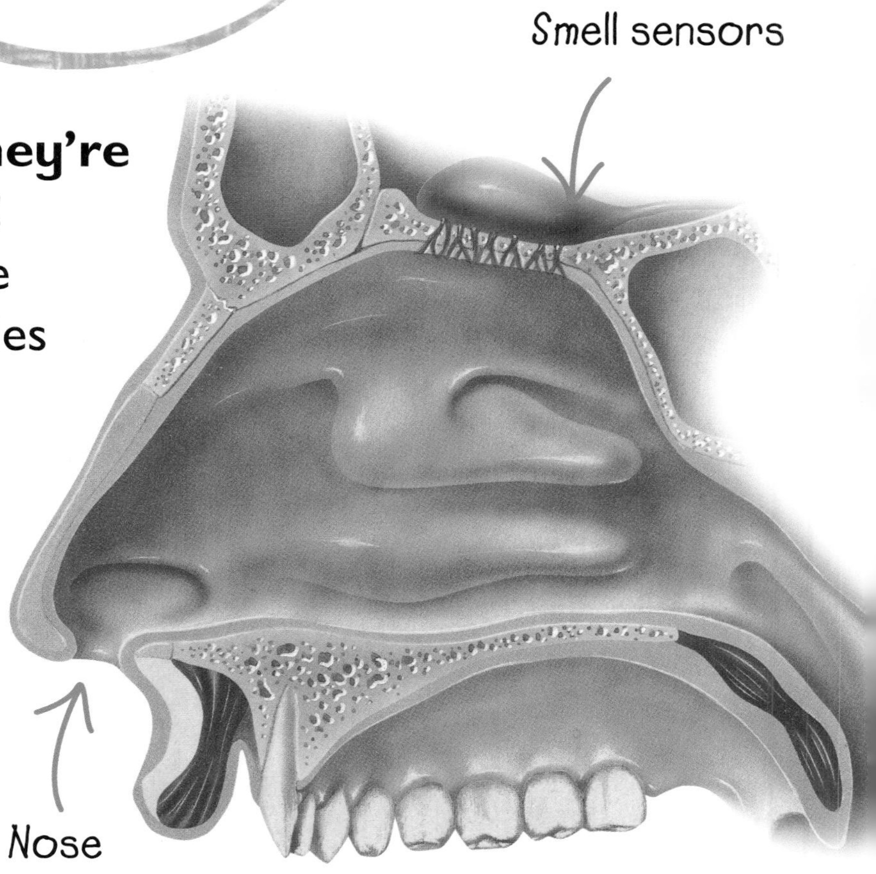

A blocked dose

Smell and taste work together when you eat. Your sense of smell helps you to taste flavours in food. When you have a cold, your smell sensors get blocked, so you cannot taste, either.

How many smells can I sense?

Your nose can sense about 3000 different smells. You don't just have a sense of smell so you can smell nice things, such as flowers and perfumes! Your sense of smell warns you if food is rotten before you eat it.

Think

Can you think of three different things that taste sour, sweet and salty?

How do I taste things?

With your tongue. Your tongue is covered with tiny taste buds. The buds sense flavours and send a signal to your brain, which tells you if something is sweet or savoury. Your tongue also moves food around your mouth and helps you to speak.

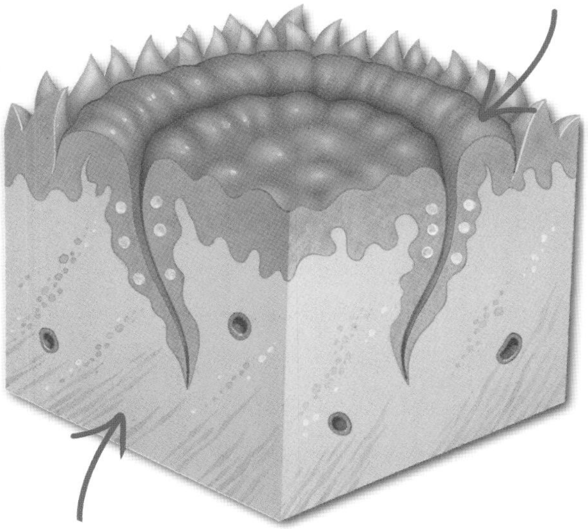

Is my brain really big?

Your brain is about the same size as your two fists put together. It is the place where you think, remember, feel happy or sad – and dream. Your brain also takes information from your senses and controls your body. The main part is called the cerebrum.

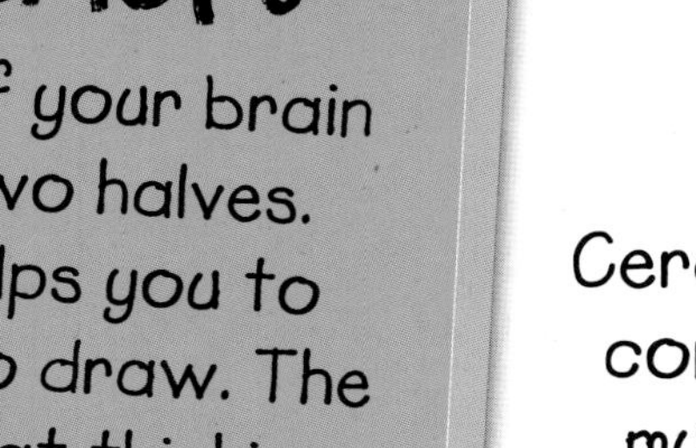

Right and left

The main part of your brain is divided into two halves. The right half helps you to play music and to draw. The left half is good at thinking.

Can my brain really wave?

Brain waves from an EEG machine

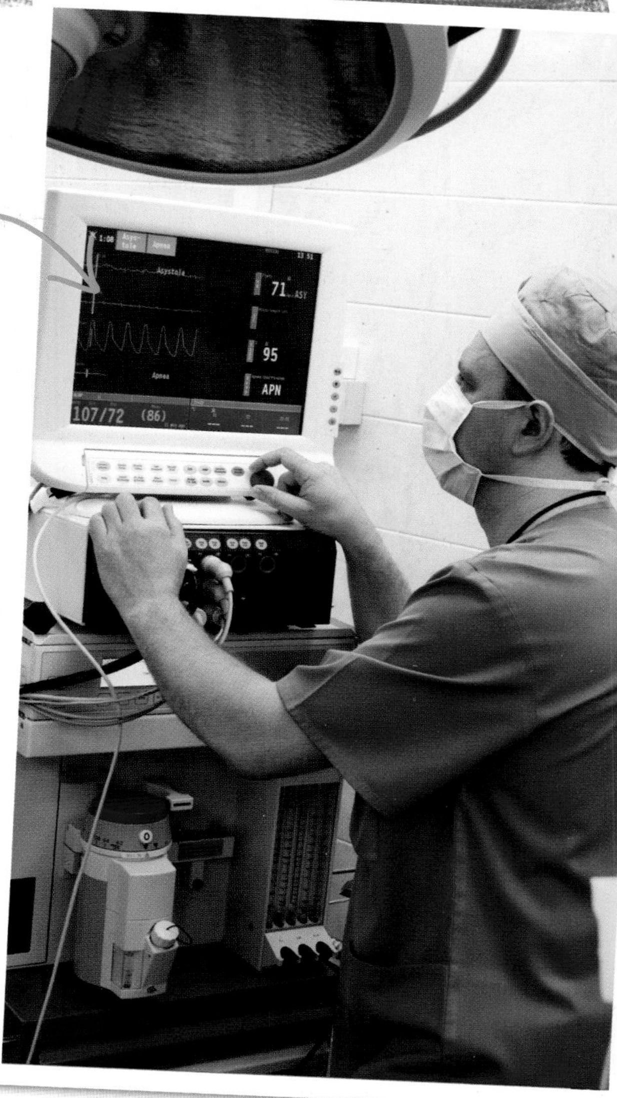

Well, sort of! Your brain works using electricity. It has about 10,000 million tiny nerve cells. Tiny bursts of electricity are always jumping around between the cells. Doctors can see your brain working by looking at the electricity with a special machine called an EEG. It shows the electricity as waves on a screen.

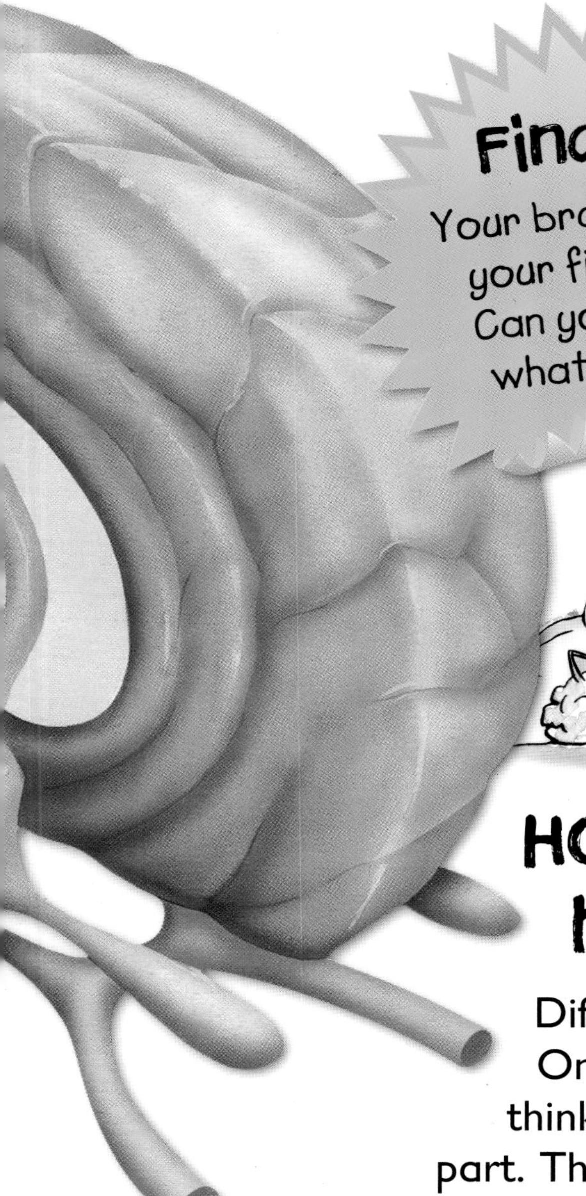

Find out

Your brain controls your five senses. Can you find out what they are?

How does my brain help me to play?

Different parts of your brain do different jobs. One part senses touch. Another part deals with thinking. Speaking is controlled by a different part. The cerebellum controls all your muscles. When you play and run, the cerebellum sends messages to your muscles to make them move.

How can I stay healthy?

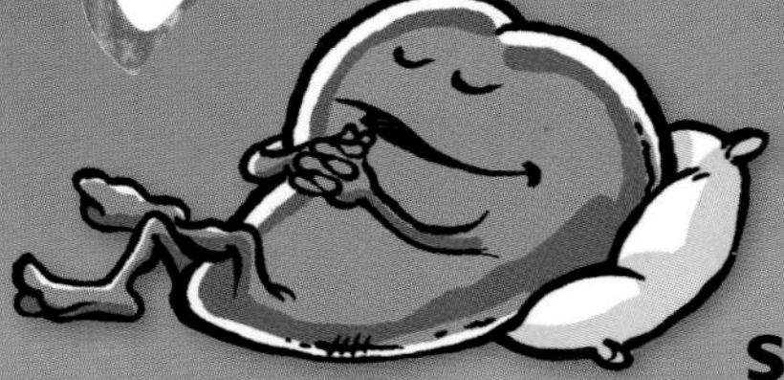

There are things you can do to stop getting ill. The easiest thing is to eat the right food your body needs, such as fruit and vegetables. Try not to eat too much salty or sugary food. Exercise, such as riding a bike will keep your bones, muscles and heart healthy.

Getting old

Your body changes as you get old. You get shorter, your skin wrinkles and your hair might go grey. But if you stay fit and healthy you could live to be 100!

What can make me sick?

Lots of things can make you sick. Illnesses such as tummy upsets are caused by germs that get into your body. You can help to stop catching germs by washing your hands before eating and after going to the toilet.

Washing your hands with hot soapy water kills germs

Why do I have injections?

All children have injections, called vaccinations, at the doctors every few years. The injections help to stop you catching serious diseases in the future. Doctors also help you to get well again when you are ill.

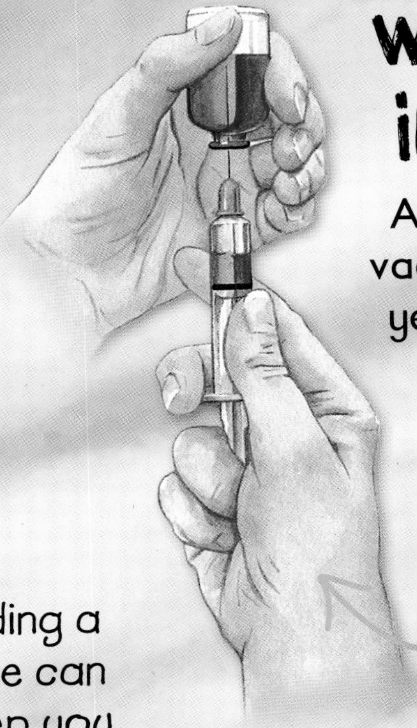

Vaccinations protect us

Riding a bike can keep you healthy

Read

What should you do before meal times and after going to the toilet? Read this page again to find out.

Quiz time

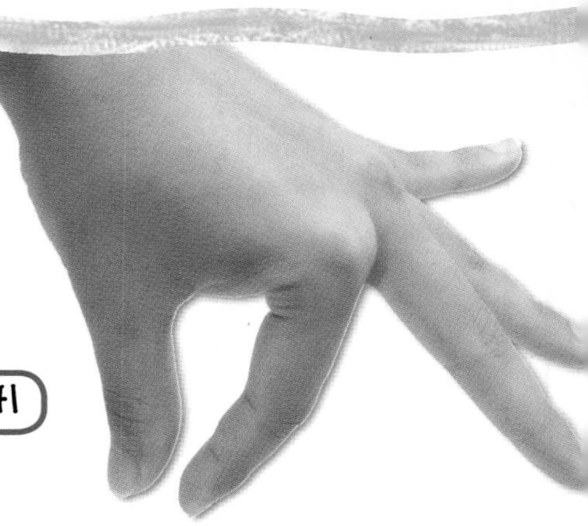

page 41

Do you remember what you have read about your body? These questions will test your memory. The pictures will help you. If you get stuck, read the pages again.

page 37

1. Am I always learning?

page 39

2. Why do I sweat when I'm warm?

3. Why do we have fingernails?

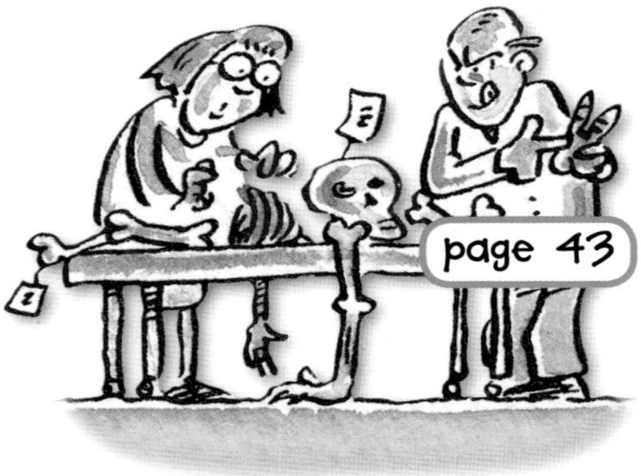

page 43

4. How are bones joined together?

5. How do muscles work?

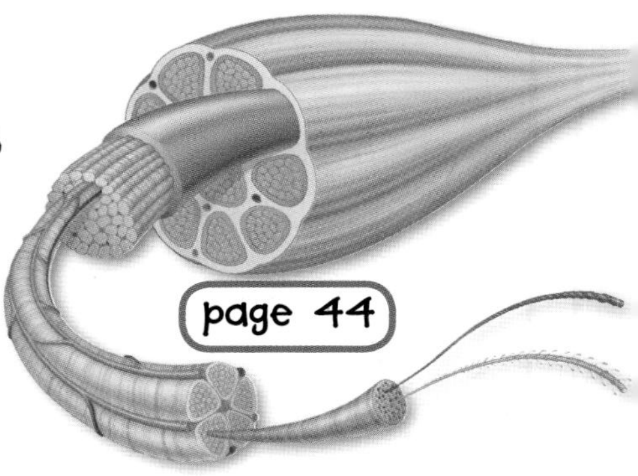

page 44

6. What makes air go into my lungs?

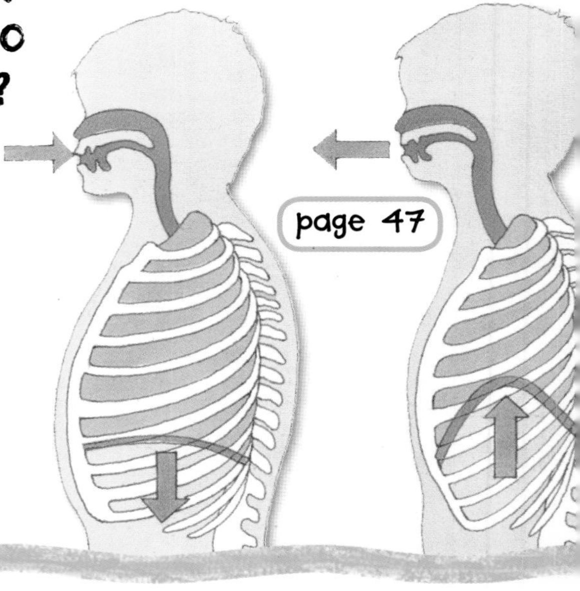

page 47

7. Why do I need to eat food?

page 49

11. Why can't I see smells?

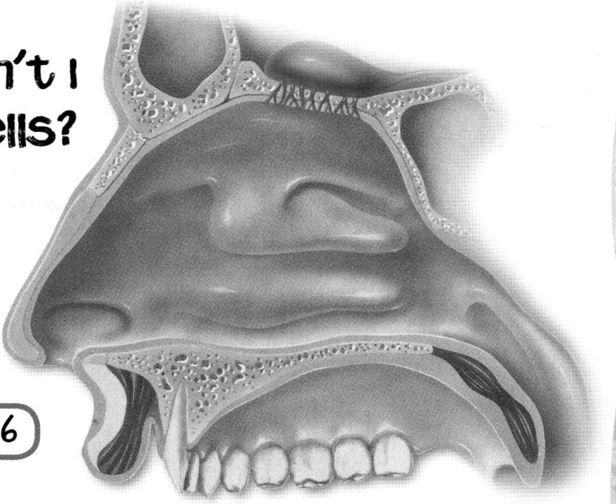

page 56

8. How many sets of teeth do I have?

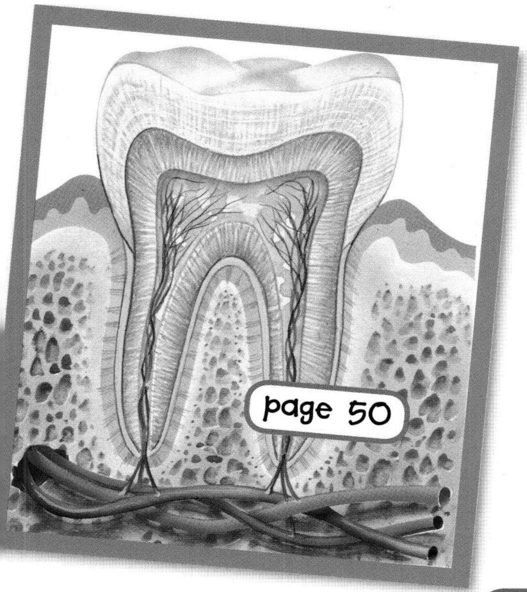

page 50

12. How does my brain help me to play?

page 59

13. What can make me sick?

page 61

9. What does blood do?

page 53

10. How do I hear sounds?

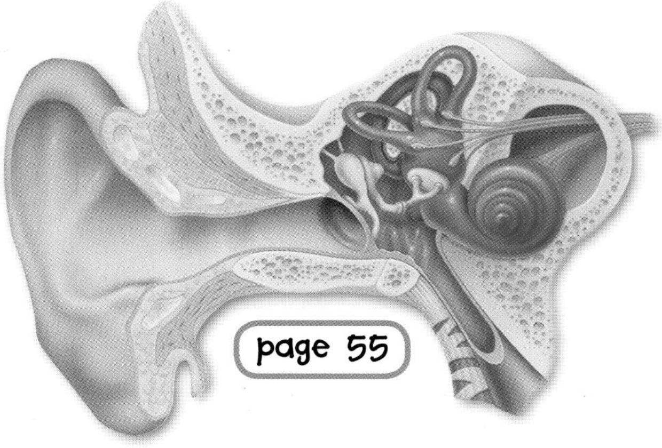

page 55

Answers

1. Yes, you are
2. To help you cool down again
3. To protect our fingertips
4. They are connected by joints
5. The fibres inside get shorter and pull
6. Muscles
7. To keep your body working
8. Two sets
9. Carries oxygen around your body
10. With the parts that are inside your ear
11. Smells are tiny particles
12. It tells your muscles to move
13. Germs

Planet Earth

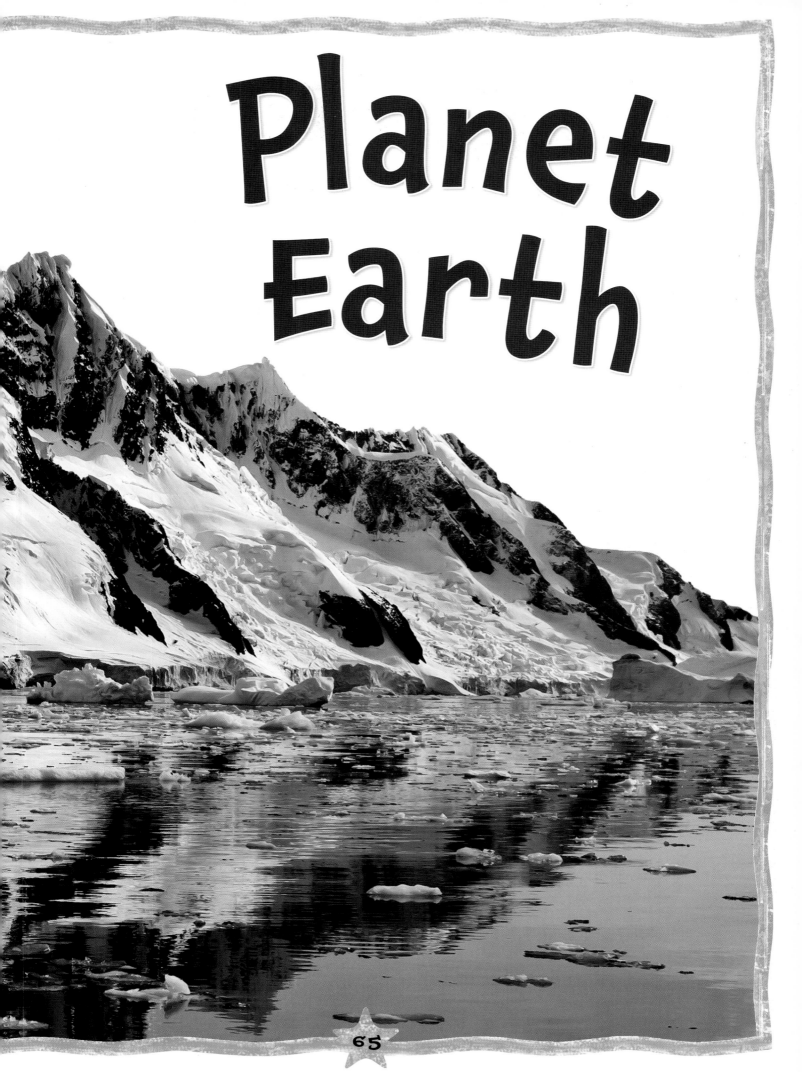

Where did the Earth come from?

The Earth came from a cloud of dust. The dust whizzed around the Sun at speed and began to stick together to form lumps of rock. The rocks crashed into each other to make planets, and one of them was the Earth.

A cloud of dust spun around the Sun
Lumps of rock began to form

Why does the Moon look lumpy?

Big rocks from space, called meteorites, have crashed into the Moon and made dents on its surface. These dents are called craters and they give the Moon a lumpy appearance.

Look

At night, use some binoculars to look at the Moon. Can you see craters on its surface?

The Earth was formed from the lumps of rock

What is the Earth made of?

The Earth is a huge ball-shaped lump of rock. Most of the Earth's surface is covered by water – this makes the seas and oceans. Rock that is not covered by water makes the land.

Face the Moon

The Moon travels around the Earth. As the Moon doesn't spin, we only ever see one side of its surface.

Why does the Earth spin?

The Earth is always spinning. This is because it was made from a spinning cloud of gas and dust. As it spins, the Earth leans a little to one side. It takes the Earth 24 hours to spin around once. This period of time is called a day.

Spinning Earth

Discover

There are 24 hours in a day. How many minutes are there in one hour?

Hot and cold

In the Caribbean, the sea can be as warm as a bath. In the Arctic, it is so cold, that often the sea freezes over.

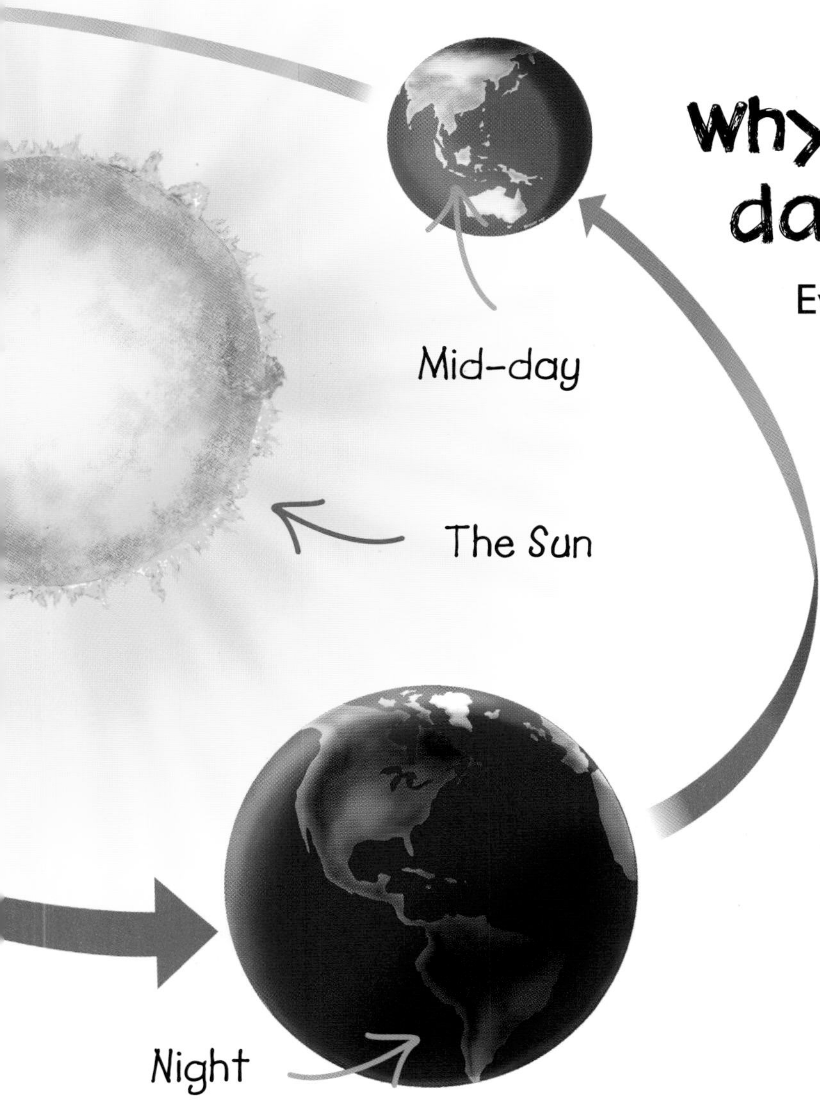

Why do we have day and night?

Every day, each part of the Earth spins towards the Sun, and then away from it. When a part of the Earth is facing the Sun, it is daytime there. When that part is facing away from Earth, it is night time.

Do people live on the Moon?

No, they don't. There is no air on the Moon so people cannot live there. Astronauts have visited the Moon in space rockets. They wear special equipment to help them breathe.

What is inside the Earth?

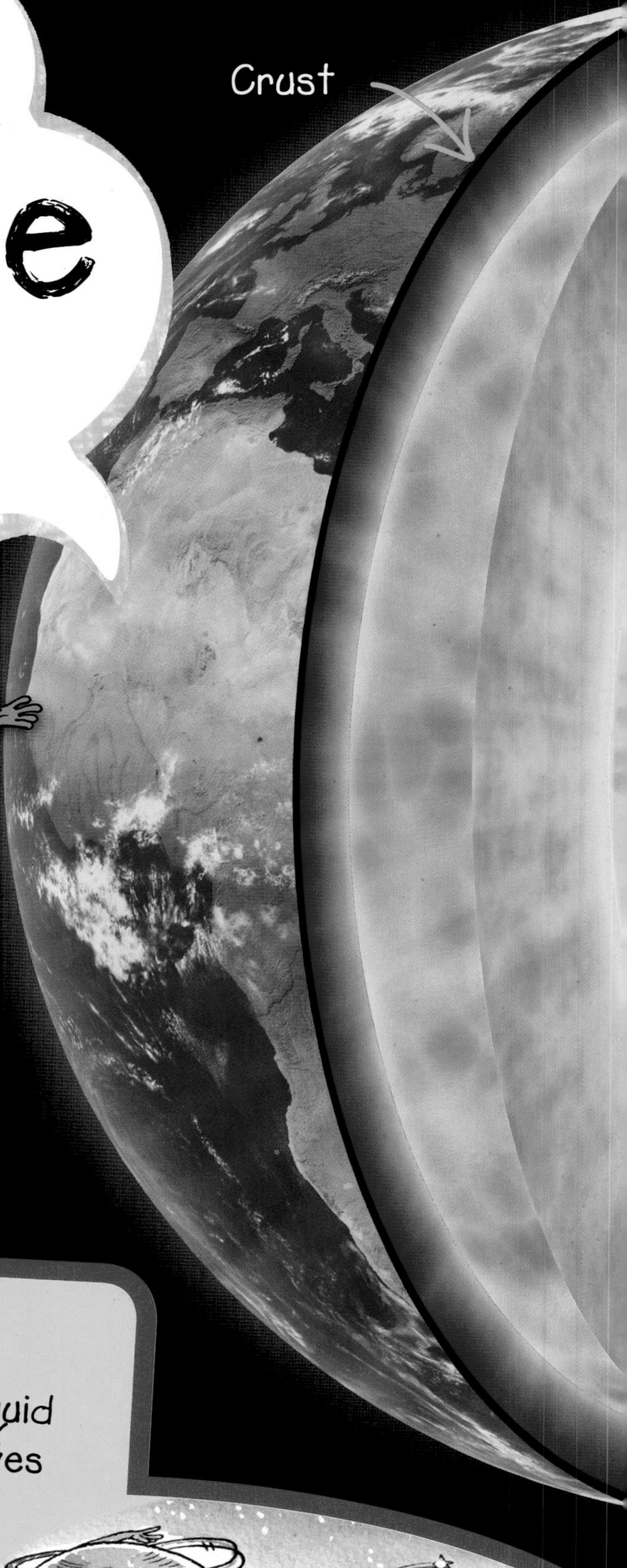

There are different layers inside the Earth. There is a thin, rocky crust, a solid area called the mantle and a centre called the core. The outer part of the core is made of hot, liquid metal. The inner core is made of solid metal.

Natural magnet

Near the centre of the Earth is hot, liquid iron. As the Earth spins, the iron behaves like a magnet. This is why a compass needle points to North and South.

Find

Use a compass to find North. Does the needle move when you do?

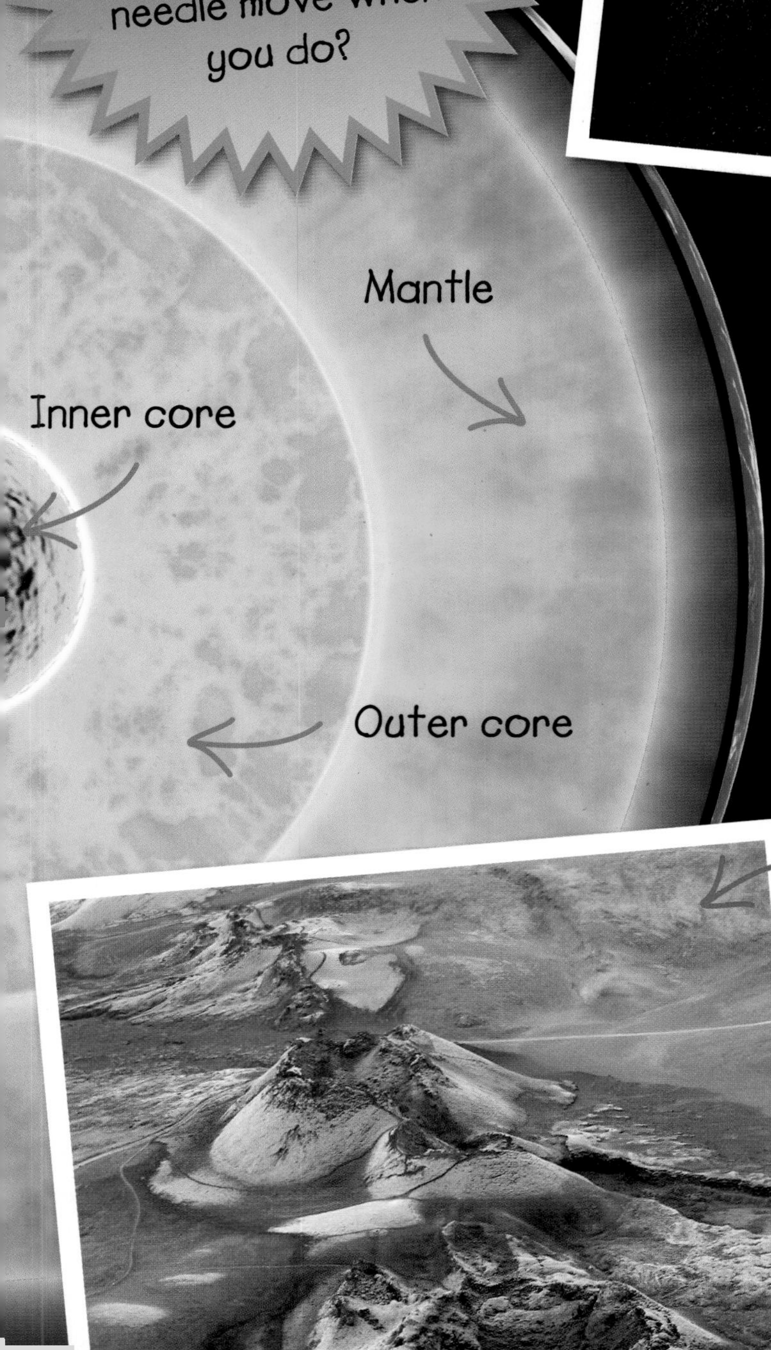

Can we travel into the Earth?

No, we can't. The Earth's core is incredibly hot and so far down that no one could ever go there. Sometimes, boiling-hot liquid rock bursts up through the Earth's surface from mountains called volcanoes.

Does the ground move?

The Earth's crust is split into huge areas called plates. Each plate is moving very slowly. If the plates move apart from each other they may cause earthquakes. If they move towards each other they may form volcanoes or mountains.

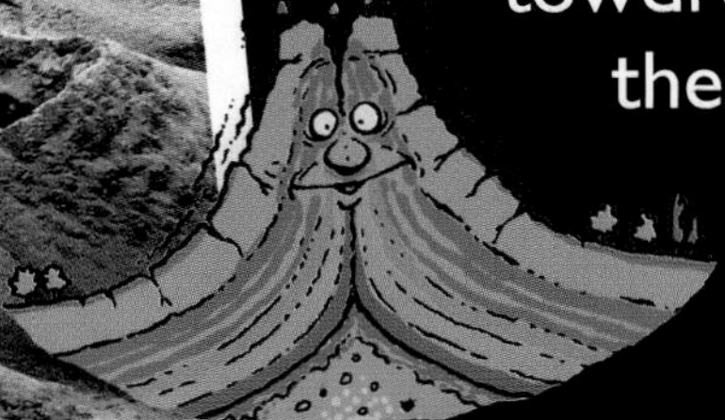

what is a fossil?

Scientists digging up and studying fossils

A fossil was once a living thing that has now turned to stone. By studying fossils, scientists can learn more about the past and how animals, such as dinosaurs, used to live.

A trilobite was an ancient sea creature

How is a fossil made?

It takes millions of years to make a fossil. When an animal dies, it may be buried by sand. The soft parts of its body rot away, leaving just bones, teeth or shells. These slowly turn to rock and a fossil forms.

Explore

Look for rocks in your garden. They may be so old, dinosaurs could have trodden on them.

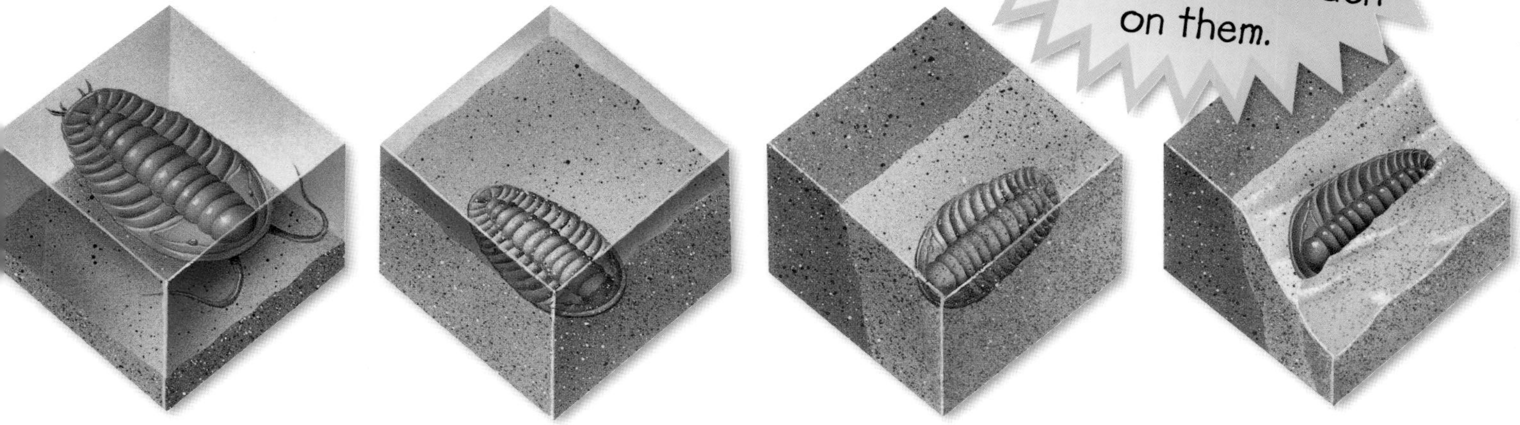

1. The trilobite dies
2. The trilobite gets covered with mud
3. The mud turns to stone
4. The fossil forms inside the stone

Cave houses

In Turkey, some people live in rocky caves. These huge cone-shaped rocks stay very cool in the hot weather.

Why do rocks crumble?

When a rock is warmed up by the Sun it gets a little bigger. When it cools down, the rock shrinks to its original size. If this process happens to a rock too often, it starts to crumble away.

What is a volcano?

A volcano is a mountain that sometimes shoots hot, liquid rock out of its top. Deep inside a volcano is an area called the magma chamber. This is filled with liquid rock. If pressure builds up in the chamber, the volcano may explode, and liquid rock will shoot out of the top.

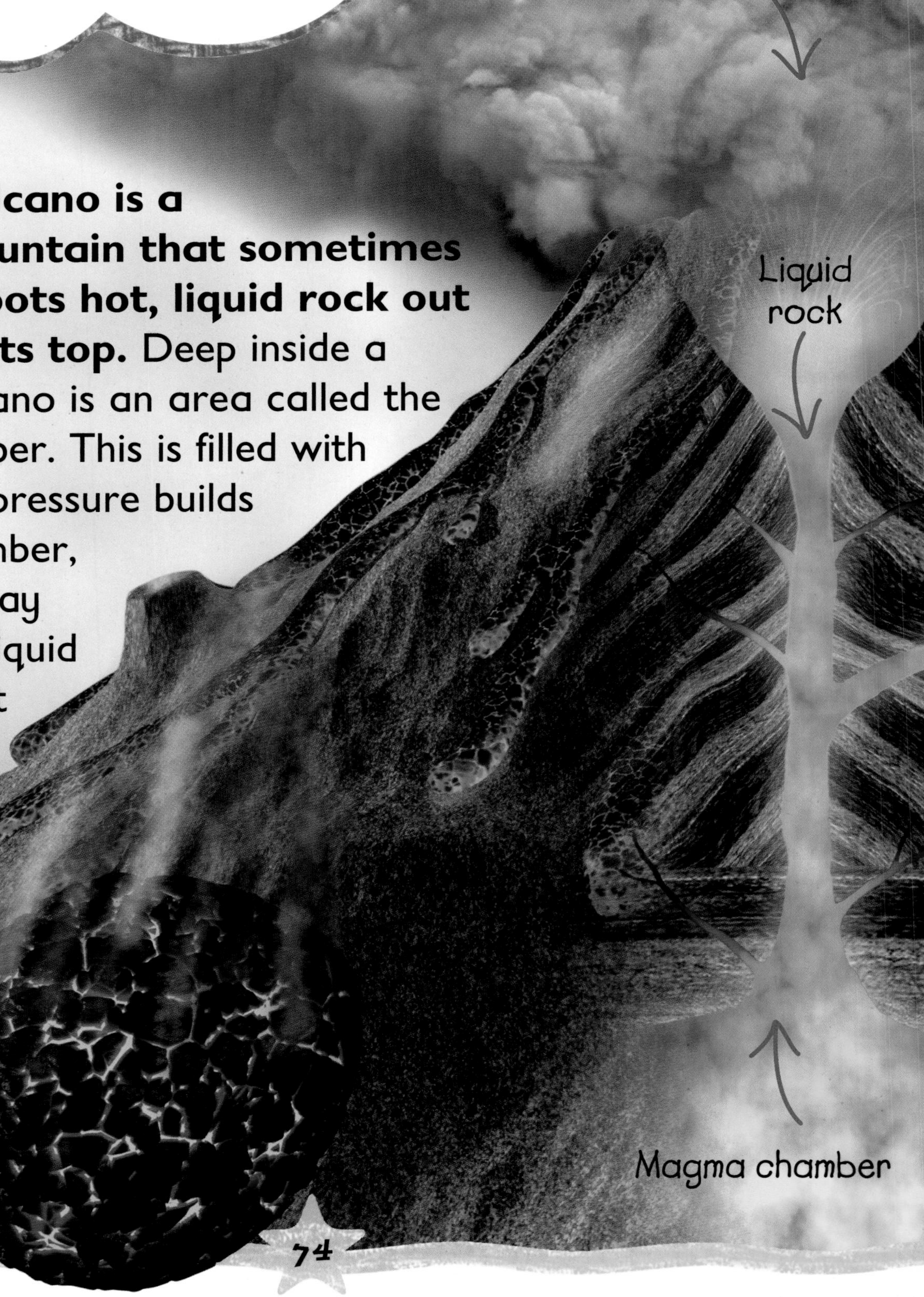

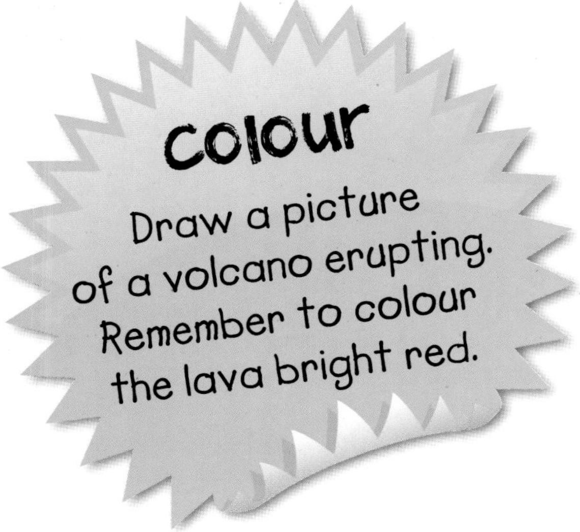

colour

Draw a picture of a volcano erupting. Remember to colour the lava bright red.

What is a range?

A range is the name for a group of mountains. The biggest ranges are the Alps in Europe, the Andes in South America, the Rockies in North America and the highest of all – the Himalayas in Asia.

How are mountains made?

One way that mountains are formed is when the Earth's plates crash together. The crust at the edge of the plates slowly crumples and folds. Over millions of years this pushes up mountains. The Himalayan Mountains in Asia were made this way.

Layer on layer

When a volcano erupts, the hot lava cools and forms a rocky layer. With each new eruption, another layer is added and the volcano gets bigger.

Why are there earthquakes?

Earthquakes happen when the plates in the Earth's crust move apart suddenly, or rub together. They start deep underground in an area called the focus. Land above the focus is shaken violently. The worst part of the earthquake happens above the focus, in an area called the epicentre.

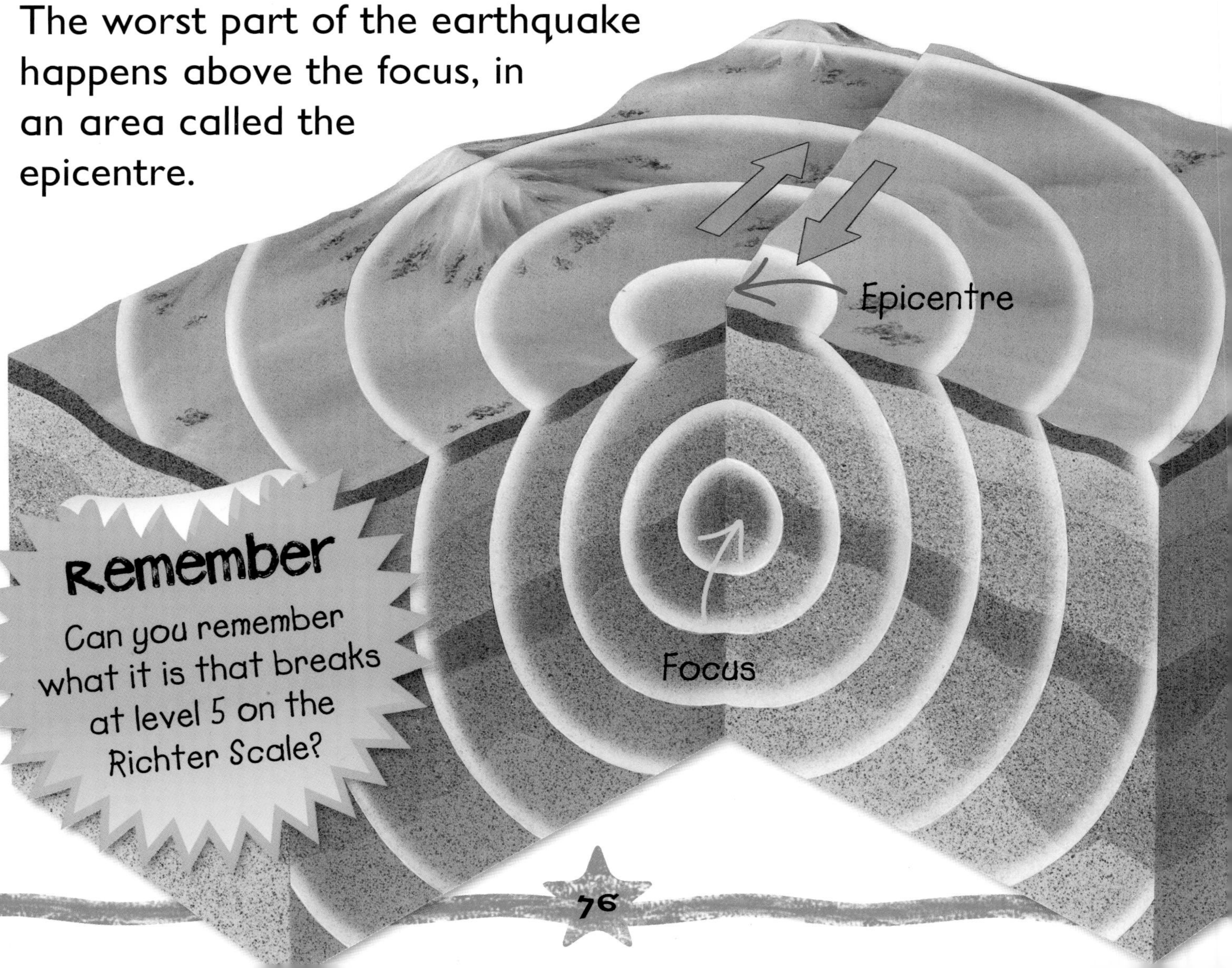

Remember

Can you remember what it is that breaks at level 5 on the Richter Scale?

What is the Richter Scale?

The Richter Scale measures the strength of an earthquake. It starts at level 1 and goes up to level 8. The higher the number, the more powerful and destructive the earthquake.

Super senses

Some people believe that animals can sense when an earthquake is about to happen!

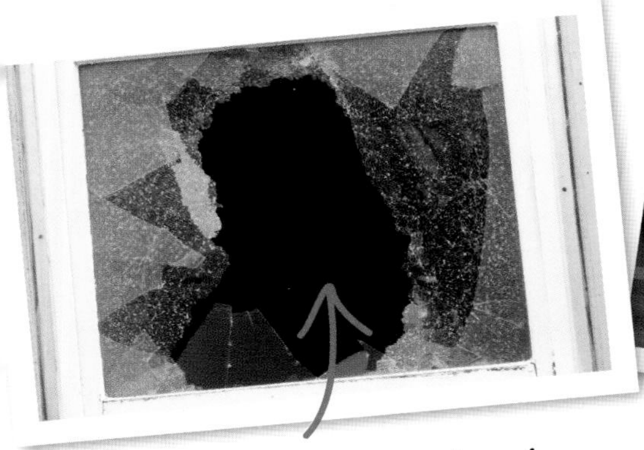

Windows break at level 5

Bridges and buildings collapse at level 7

Widespread destruction at level 8

Can earthquakes start fires?

Yes, a powerful earthquake can cause fires. In 1906, a huge earthquake in San Francisco, USA caused lots of fires. The fires burnt down most of the city and the people who lived there became homeless.

What is a glacier?

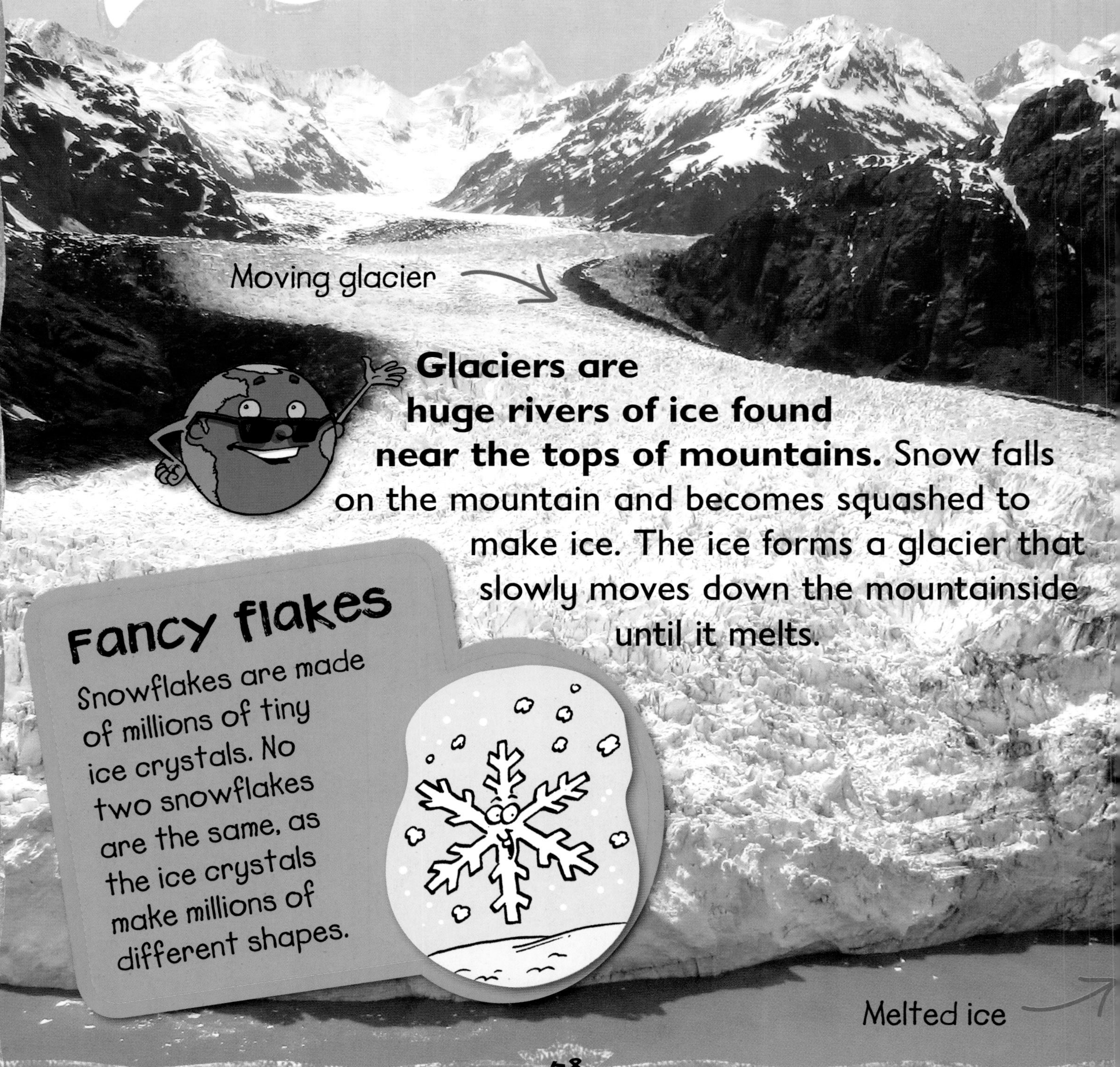

Glaciers are huge rivers of ice found near the tops of mountains. Snow falls on the mountain and becomes squashed to make ice. The ice forms a glacier that slowly moves down the mountainside until it melts.

Fancy flakes

Snowflakes are made of millions of tiny ice crystals. No two snowflakes are the same, as the ice crystals make millions of different shapes.

Can ice be fun?

Yes, it can! Many people go ice skating and they wear special boots with blades on them called ice skates. Figure skaters are skilled athletes who compete to win prizes.

Look

Next time it snows, put some gloves on and let the snowflakes fall into your hand. Can you see crystals?

What is an iceberg?

Icebergs are big chunks of ice that have broken off glaciers and drifted into the sea. Only a small part of the iceberg can be seen above the water. The main part of the iceberg is hidden under the water.

Where do rivers flow to?

Rivers flow to the sea or into lakes. They start off as small streams in hills and mountains. The streams flow downhill, getting bigger and wider. The place where a river meets the sea, or flows into a lake, is called the river mouth.

Discover

Try to find out the name of the highest waterfall in the world. Where is it?

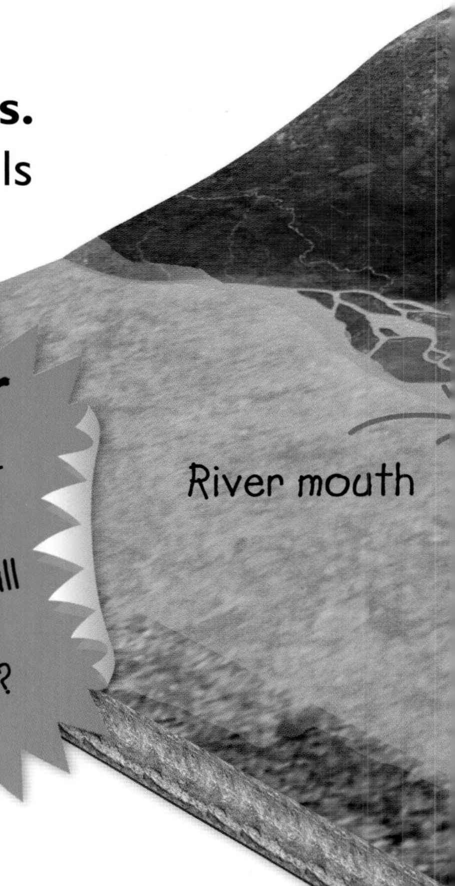

River mouth

Waterfall

Why are there waterfalls?

Waterfalls are made when water wears down rocks to make a cliff face. The water then falls over the edge into a deep pool called a plunge pool. Waterfalls may only be a few centimetres high, or several hundred metres high!

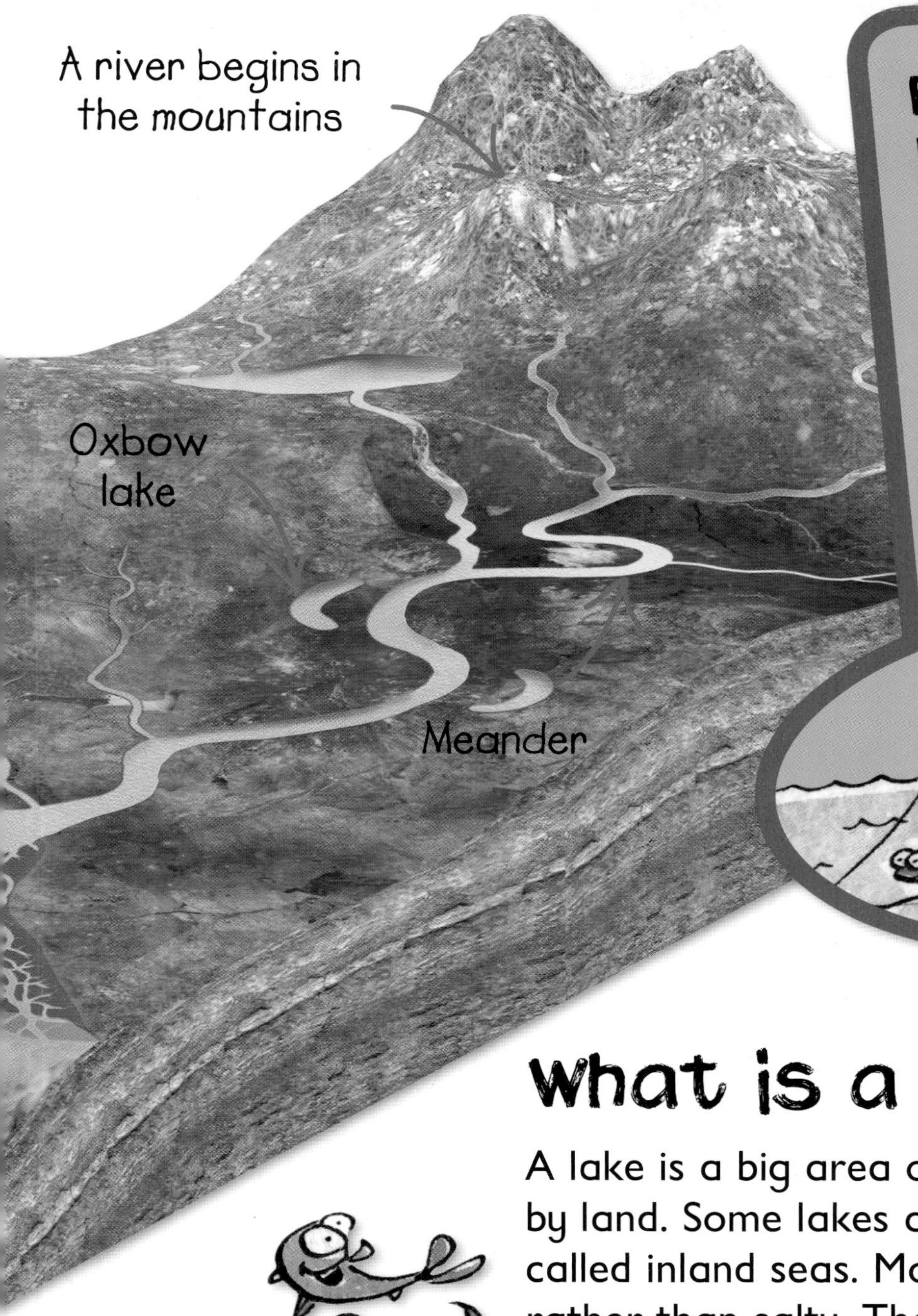

Risky business

Salmon are a type of fish. Every year, fishermen try to catch them as they swim back to the river they were born in to have their babies.

What is a lake?

A lake is a big area of water that is surrounded by land. Some lakes are so big that they are called inland seas. Most lake water is fresh rather than salty. The biggest lake in the world is the Caspian Sea in Asia.

Are there mountains under the sea?

Yes, there are. Mountains lie hidden in very deep oceans. The ocean floor is very flat and is called a plain. Large mountain ranges may rise across the plain. Some oceans even have underwater volcanoes.

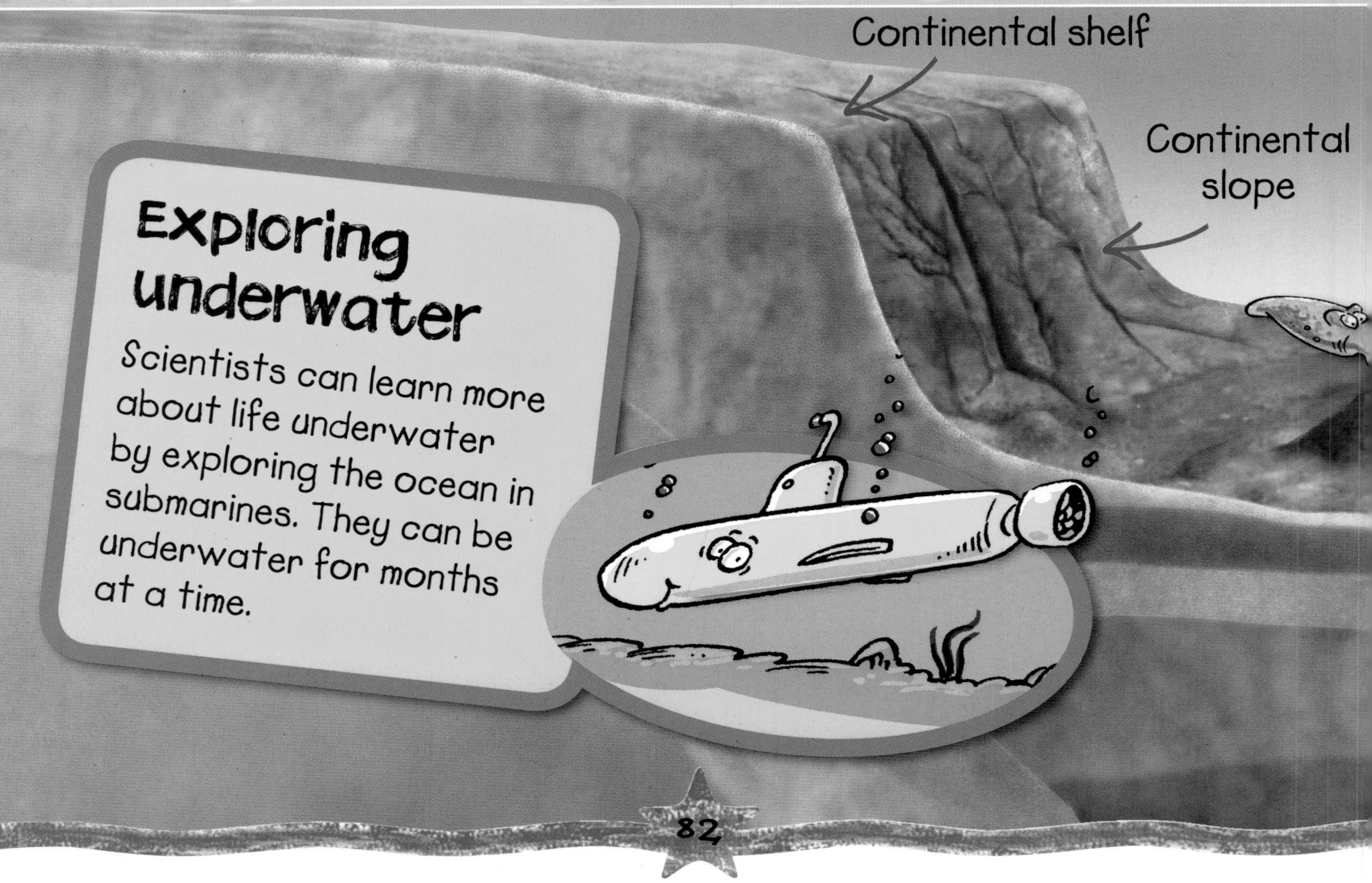

Exploring underwater

Scientists can learn more about life underwater by exploring the ocean in submarines. They can be underwater for months at a time.

Why do coasts change?

The coast is where the land meets the sea, and it is always changing. In many places, waves crash onto land and rocks, slowly breaking them up. This can change the shape of the coastline.

What is coral?

Coral is made from polyps. These are tiny creatures the size of pin heads that live in warm, shallow waters. The polyps join together in large groups and create rocky homes. These are called coral reefs.

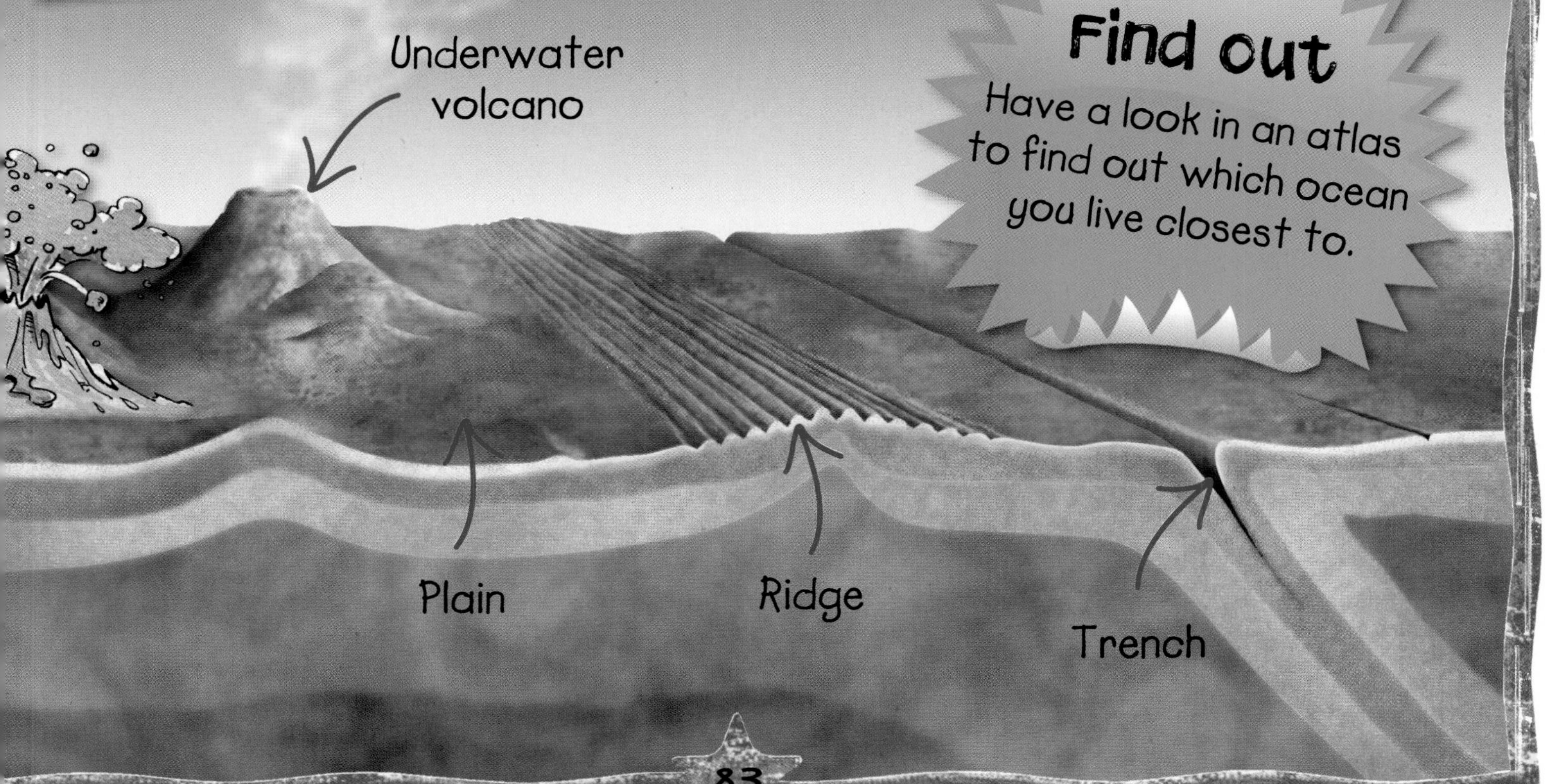

Find out

Have a look in an atlas to find out which ocean you live closest to.

How are caves made?

When rain falls on rock, it can make caves. Rainwater mixes with a gas in the air called carbon dioxide. This makes a strong acid. The acid can attack the rock and make it disappear. Underground, the rainwater makes caves in which streams and lakes can be found.

Can lava make caves?

When a volcano erupts and lava flows through the mountain, it can carve out a cave. A long time after the eruption, when the volcano is no longer active, people can walk through this lava cave without having to bend down.

Lava cave

Stalactites

Stalagmites

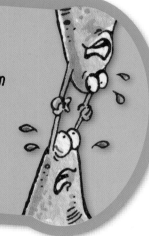

Super spiky

Stalagmites grow up from the cave floor. Dripping water leaves a rocky substance that grows into a rocky spike.

What is a stalactite?

Rocky spikes that hang from cave ceilings are called stalactites. When water drips from the cave ceiling, it leaves tiny amounts of a rocky substance behind. Very slowly, over a long period of time, this grows into a stalactite.

Remember

Stalactites hold on tight, stalagmites might reach the top!

Is there water in the desert?

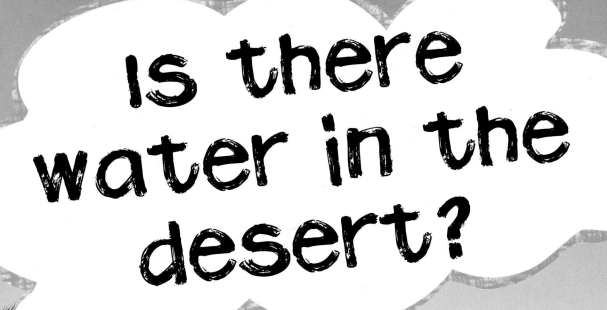

Yes, there is. Deserts sometimes get rain. This rainwater seeps into the sand and collects in rock. The water then builds up and forms a pool called an oasis. Plants grow around the oasis and animals visit the pool to drink.

What are grasslands?

Grasslands are found when there is too much rain for a desert but not enough rain for a forest. Large numbers of animals can be found living and feeding on grasslands, including zebras, antelopes and lions.

What is a rainforest?

In hot places, such as South America, there are areas of thick, green forest. These are rainforests, and they are home to amazing plants and animals. Rainforests have rainy weather all year round.

Draw

Create a picture of a camel crossing a desert. Don't forget to include its wide feet!

Hummingbirds like this one live in rainforests

Oasis

Big feet

Camels have wide feet that stop them sinking into the sand. They can also store water in their bodies for a long time.

Where does rain come from?

Rain comes from the ocean! Water moves between the ocean, air and land in a water cycle. A fine mist of water rises into the air from the ocean and from plants. This fine mist then forms clouds. Water can fall from the clouds as rain.

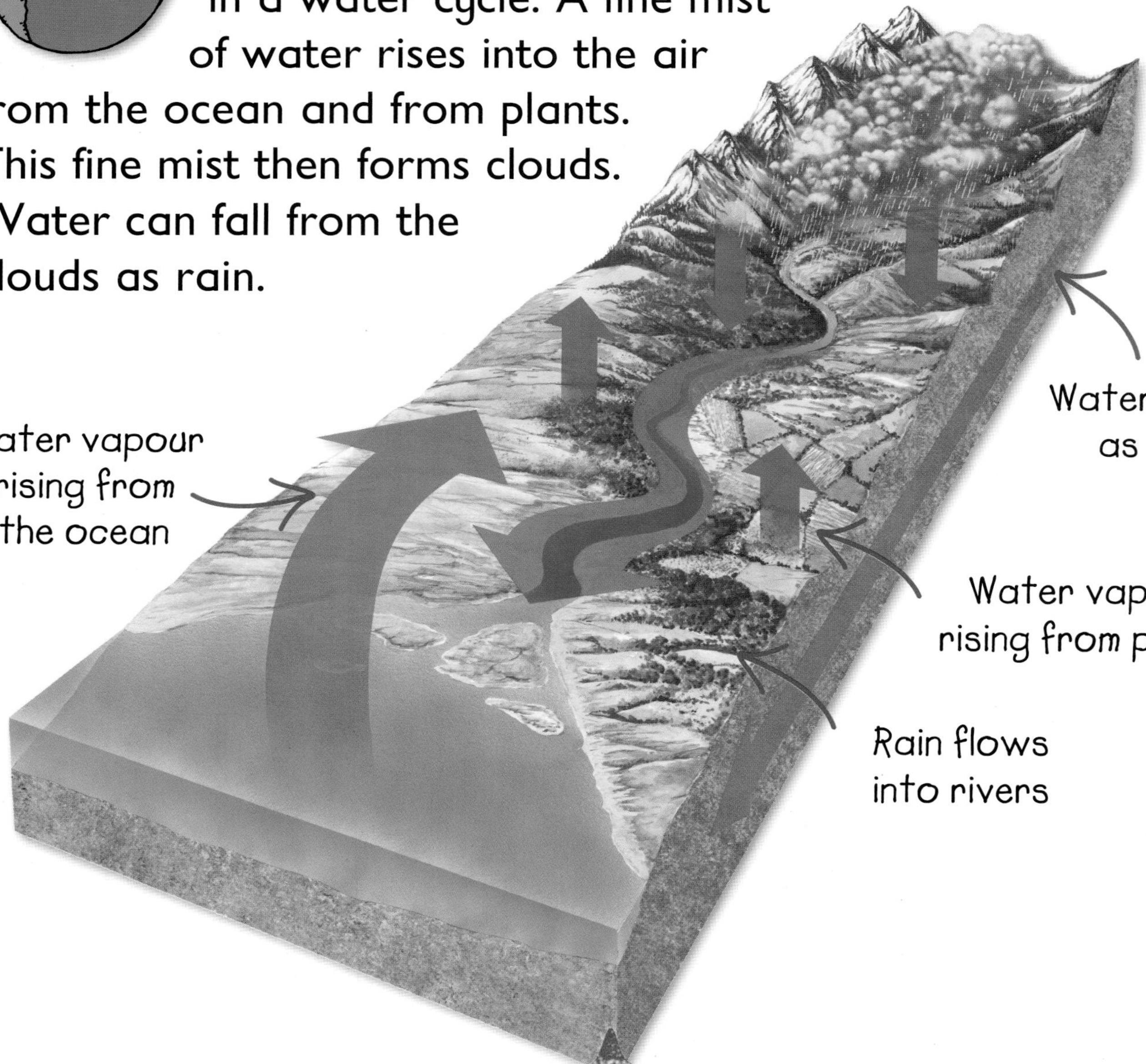

Stormy weather

Every day there are more than 45,000 thunderstorms on the Earth! Thunderstorms are most common in tropical places, such as Indonesia.

Pretend

Spin around as fast as you can and pretend to be a tornado. You will get very dizzy!

Tornado

How does a tornado start?

A tornado is the fastest wind on Earth. Tornadoes start over very hot ground. Here, warm air rises quickly and makes a spinning funnel. This funnel acts like a vacuum cleaner, destroying buildings and lifting cars and lorries off the ground.

Do storms have eyes?

Yes, storms do have eyes! A hurricane is a very dangerous storm. The centre of a hurricane is called the eye and here it is completely still. However, the rest of the storm can reach speeds of up to 300 kilometres an hour.

How can we help the Earth?

Some of the things that people do can damage the Earth. Factories pump chemicals into the air and water. Forests are being cut down, killing the wildlife that lives there, and fumes from cars are clogging up the air. Scientists are trying to find new ways to protect the Earth before it is too late.

Help

Save all of your empty drinks cans and bottles and take them to your recycling centre.

Save the planet

There are lots of things we can do to protect our planet. Recycling, picking up litter, switching lights off and walking to the shops all help to make a difference.

How can we protect our planet?

Large areas of land have been made into national parks where wildlife is protected. People can go there to learn about both plants and animals.

Pond dipping

Wind turbines

What is renewable energy?

Burning coal and oil creates pollution, and in time these fuels will run out. Scientists are developing ways of using energy sources, such as wind, which replenish themselves naturally.

Quiz time

Do you remember what you have read about planet Earth? These questions will test your memory. The pictures will help you. If you get stuck, read the pages again.

page 66

1. Why does the Moon look lumpy?

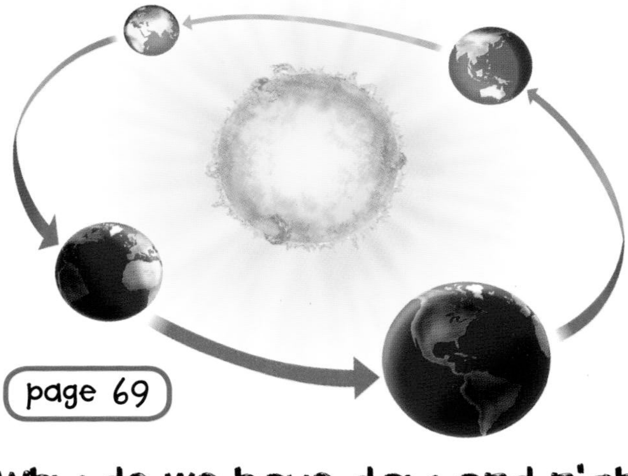

page 69

2. Why do we have day and night?

3. What is inside the Earth?

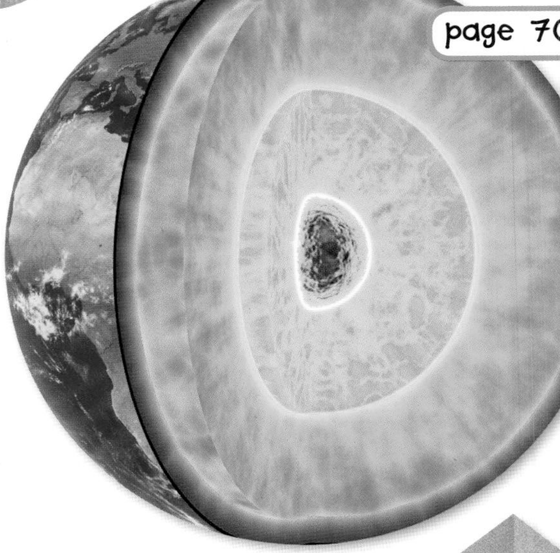

page 70

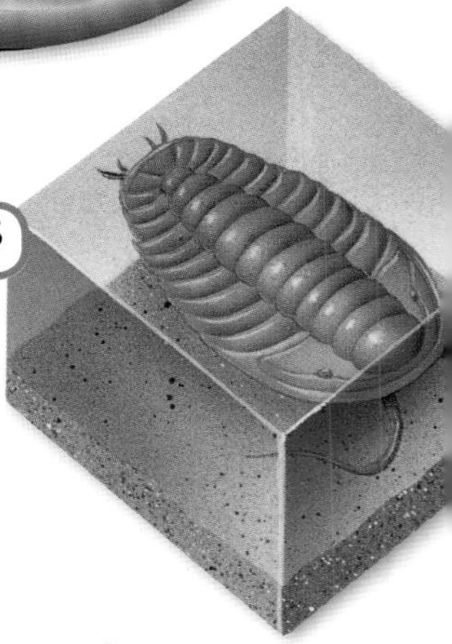

page 73

4. How is a fossil made?

5. What is a range?

page 75

6. What is the Richter scale?

page 77

7. Can ice be fun?

page 79

8. What is an iceberg?

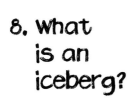

page 79

9. Why are there waterfalls?

page 80

10. Can lava make caves?

page 85

11. What is a stalactite?

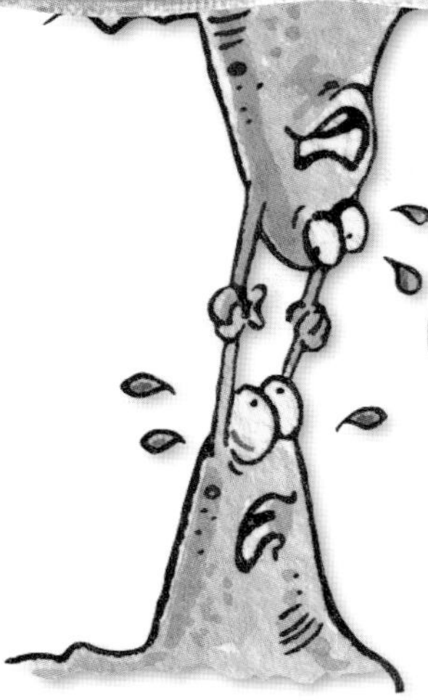

page 85

12. What is a rainforest?

page 87

13. Do storms have eyes?

page 89

Answers

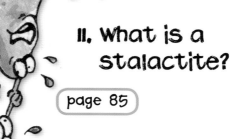

1. Because there are craters on its surface
2. Because the Earth is always spinning
3. Lots of different layers of rock and metal
4. By turning an animal's hard parts to rock over millions of years
5. A group of mountains
6. It measures the strength of an earthquake
7. Yes, people skate on ice for fun
8. A big chunk of ice that has broken off a glacier
9. Because water flows over cliffs
10. Yes it can
11. A rocky spike that hangs from the ceiling of a cave
12. A large, thick, green forest that grows in a hot place
13. Yes, the centre of a hurricane is called the eye

Index

S

T

U

V

W

X